PROPELLER

US ARMY TWIN BEECHES

Terry Love

Schiffer Publishing Ltd
4880 Lower Valley Road • Atglen, PA 19310

Other Schiffer Books by the Author:
Wings of Air America: A Photo History, ISBN: 978-0-7643-0619-8
The Republic Airlines Story: An Illustrated History, 1945-1986,
ISBN: 978-0-7643-4247-9

Other Schiffer Books on Related Subjects:
Twin Cessna: The Cessna 300 and 400 Series of Light Twins,
Ron Smith, ISBN: 978-0-7643-5226-3

Library of Congress Control Number: 2017931643

Designed by Molly Shields
Type set in Square721 BT/Times New Roman

ISBN: 978-0-7643-5295-9
Printed in China

Published by Schiffer Publishing, Ltd.
4880 Lower Valley Road
Atglen, PA 19310
Phone: (610) 593-1777; Fax: (610) 593-2002
E-mail: Info@schifferbooks.com
Web: www.schifferbooks.com

For our complete selection of fine books on this and related subjects, please visit our website at www.schifferbooks.com. You may also write for a free catalog.

Schiffer Publishing's titles are available at special discounts for bulk purchases for sales promotions or premiums. Special editions, including personalized covers, corporate imprints, and excerpts, can be created in large quantities for special needs. For more information, contact the publisher.

We are always looking for people to write books on new and related subjects. If you have an idea for a book, please contact us at proposals@schifferbooks.com.

CONTENTS

ACKNOWLEDGMENTS

This book is dedicated to CW3 Andrew McAdams, Sgt. Drew Scobie, and Kristopher Noble, the crew of an MC-12S (call sign Pursue 46) shot down and killed on January 10, 2014, over Afghanistan in support of Task Force ODIN. Also to Capt. Michael Marker, WO1 Harold Algaard, SP/6 John Strawn, SP/5 Richard Hentz, and SP/5 Rodney Osborne, shot down and killed over North Vietnam on March 4, 1971 (call sign Vanguard 216 of the 138th Aviation Company in LEFT JAB JU-21A, serial number 67-18063). Finally, to WO1 Milton W. Smith and WO1 Jonathan P. Shaffer, whose RU-8D crashed on takeoff on December 29, 1967, in Vietnam while assigned to the 138th Aviation Company. Special thanks go to Ray Wilhite and Mark Nankivil of the St. Louis Aviation Museum and to the Kansas Aviation Museum in Wichita, Kansas, the home of Beechcraft.

INTRODUCTION

Walter Beech was born in 1891 on a farm near Pulaski, Tennessee. Mechanical things became a way of life for him at an early age. At fourteen Walter built his own glider, which he designed. He then soloed in a Curtiss biplane pusher. When WWI came along, Walter joined the US Army and earned the rank of sergeant in November 1917. He was initially assigned to Kelly Field, Texas, but was reassigned to Rich Field, near Waco, in early 1918. Contrary to myth, Beech did not learn to fly, nor was he a flight instructor during the war. He overhauled and supervised repair of airplane engines installed in the Curtiss and de Havilland biplanes used to train new pilots.

When the Armistice was signed in November 1918, Walter decided to remain in the Army. His persistence paid off. He was chosen as a pilot candidate and became an enlisted airman in October 1919. With funding for an air service slashed by a peace-conscious Congress, Beech left the Army and began flying for the Williams-Hill Airplane Company in Arkansas City, Kansas.

In 1921, he traveled to nearby Wichita and was hired to fly for the Wichita Laird Airplane Company, led by famous E. M. "Matty" Laird. Although a pilot of limited experience, Walter slowly became much more proficient, and by 1922 had earned a reputation in the Midwest as a daredevil aviator. Laird felt that Beech's 250 hours of flying experience was not enough, and Laird was not surprised when Beech crashed a Swallow shortly after being hired. Beech soon developed into a skilled race pilot and began earning the company money in regional air races.

The name of the company was changed to Swallow Airplane Company and Beech became the chief pilot for them. Beech resigned in 1925, and along with Lloyd Stearman persuaded Clyde Cessna to join a new company called Travel Air. Beech became president of the company. He hired Olive Ann Mellor as his secretary; they later married. She eventually became the "power behind the throne" just after Walter's death in 1950. Clyde Cessna

The prototype Beech Bonanza (NX80040) flew for the first time on December 22, 1945. It was the basis for the Beech Twin Bonanza, which followed a few years later. The Bonanza is still in production more than seventy years after it made its first flight. This is by far the longest produced aircraft in the world. *Kansas Aviation Museum*

and Lloyd Stearman eventually left and started their own airplane companies.

Travel Air became a major player in the world's production of aircraft just before the Depression hit. Beech sold the company to Curtiss-Wright and moved to Buffalo, New York, to work with Curtiss-Wright. He soon moved back to Wichita, Kansas, as he did not like living back east in New York.

Beech then started Beech Aircraft Corporation on April 1, 1932. The first project he did was the magnificent Beech Model 17 Staggerwing. This model is still highly prized today after 780 Model 17 Staggerwings were built in the middle of the Depression. Models 1 through 16 were all Travel Air (which became part of the Curtiss-Wright Corporation) designations. In 1937, the Beech Model 18 came along. It was built very strong, like all Beech aircraft. This became the C-45/SNB series of aircraft.

During WWII more than 7,400 C-45/SNB series were built, and more than 90% of the US Army Air Force's navigator/bombardiers and more than 50% of USAAF multi-engine pilots learned on this series of aircraft.

By 1944, Beech began thinking about postwar aircraft. He wanted an all-metal high-speed business aircraft for four passengers. His friend (who left and started his own aircraft firm) Clyde Cessna recognized the same market, and what emerged was the Beech Model 35 Bonanza and the Cessna 195. With its high-wing, seven-cylinder radial engine, fixed tail wheel undercarriage, and roll-down side windows, the Cessna 195 was little more than a continuation of prewar technology.

The Beech Model 35 was designed to meet Walter Beech's requests for an aircraft that could carry four people and their luggage in car-like comfort at 180 mph. Beech engineers had just finished work on the Beech XA-38 Grizzly attack aircraft.

The Beech Model 35 Bonanza was a fighter-based aircraft featuring a horizontally opposed six-cylinder engine, streamlined shape, retractable landing gear with a nose gear, a low-wing configuration, and a distinctive V-shaped tail. When Beech was designing the Bonanza, the "hottest" fighter around was the North American P-51 Mustang, so Beech adopted the laminar flow wing and wing planform from the Mustang. This shape of the wing is still used in the latest versions of the C-12 series today. Beech made the right decisions, because the Bonanza is still in production more than seventy years later and more than 17,000 have been built. It has been in continuous production longer than any other airplane in history. The first flight of a Bonanza was on December 22, 1945, by Vern L. Carsten. The registration of the prototype Bonanza was NX80150. The Bonanza Type Certificate is in the Utility category, and was intended for limited aerobatic operations.

The next project after the successful launch of the Bonanza would be a twin-engine version called the Twin Bonanza. Walter Beech died in 1950, and his wife, Olive, took over the running of the corporation. She became one of the first women to run a large corporation in America. She was very successful running Beechcraft Corporation. She retired in 1980, after thirty years as the CEO of Beechcraft.

CHAPTER ONE

C-45 EXPEDITOR

By the late 1930s, Beechcraft management had identified a market for their new design named the Model 18. It would have civilian and military applications. The design was conventional for the time, including radial engines, all-metal semi-monocoque construction with fabric-covered control surfaces, and a tail wheel. It was designed to have low operating costs, cabin comfort, and safety comparable to that found on airliners. Also considered was the ability to operate from small airfields, plus a high degree of reliability and ease of maintenance. Design work began in December 1935.

The first aircraft rolled out in January 1937. For the maiden flight, a pilot from Transcontinental & Western Airlines (TWA), James N. Payton, was selected because he was familiar with two-engine aircraft. H. C. "Ding" Rankin, a Beech test pilot, was the co-pilot. The first flight took place on January 15, 1937, in Wichita, Kansas. It was highly successful and uneventful. The airplane cruised at about 200 mph and a range of more than 1,000 miles, and it was priced at about $30,000.

Noting that it was a little underpowered, Beech removed the two 320 hp R-760 engines and replaced them with the very reliable Pratt & Whitney R-985 with 450 hp each. This increased the cruising speed to around 225 mph. This version first flew in January 1940 with H. C. "Ding" Rankin at the controls and Walter Beech as copilot. They won the MacFadden Trophy when they flew from St. Louis, Missouri, to Miami, Florida, at an average speed of 234 mph. On this model, aerodynamic drag was reduced with the introduction of flush riveting.

Eleven Model 18s were purchased by the USAAC, with the first aircraft being delivered on February 29, 1940. It became the UC-45B. The second military variant was the UC-45A; twenty were delivered between March and August 1940.

Nearly 8,000 were built in a production run of about thirty-three years. The last Model 18 came off the assembly line on November 26, 1969. A little over half of those built (4,526) went to the Army (as C-45s/AT-11s) and Navy (as SNBs).

In 1951, the C-45 went through a major rebuilding program. These remanufactured aircraft were redesignated C-45G with new military serial numbers. Modifications included a heavier wing section truss structure, new landing gear struts, wheels, brakes, and instrument panel, and new constant speed fully feathering propellers. They were utilized for a variety of purposes, but were mainly utilitarian. About thirty different countries' militaries operated the Beech Model 18. The last US Air Force C-45 was phased out in November 1963. The US Navy retired its last SNB-5 in July 1972.

Following the Korean War the Army was procuring the L-23A Seminole in numbers, but there were numerous Beech C-45/SNBs in storage. As a money-saving choice, the US Army obtained some of these from storage even though there was no procurement for them. The total number of C-45 aircraft obtained by the Army over the years was forty-seven.

The obtained aircraft were a variety of models of the Beech C-45/SNB series. Beginning in 1956, twenty-six ex-US Navy SNB-2s and JRBs were utilized by the US Army. One of the forty-seven obtained (SNB-5P [RC-45J] BuNo 12375) was a photo-reconnaissance trainer. The aircraft was used by the Army to develop airborne intelligence-gathering systems and techniques. During its career with the Army, this C-45 was equipped with various cameras and ELINT sensors. Some of the sensors included the prototypes for the LEFT JAB and LEFT FOOT systems.

BuNo 23783 was based at Fort Polk, Louisiana, while BuNo 29637 was assigned to New Cumberland Army Depot and later to the Lackland AFB Museum in USAF markings. BuNo 29637 flew with the Army, Navy, and Air Force. BuNo 39935 was assigned to Fort Benning Infantry Center, and BuNo 51238 was at the US Army School at Fort Gordon, Georgia. BuNo 51228 wore Department of the Army markings. BuNo 51288 had Yuma Proving Ground markings, while BuNo67166 had Atlanta Army Depot markings and BuNo89493 wore Alabama Army National Guard markings.

Some C-45s were converted to Volpar tricycle landing gear versions; the Army obtained seven of them. BuNo 23824 had JFK Center for Special Warfare markings and BuNo51312 wore Anniston Depot on it. BuNos 23829 and 39829 were both test bed aircraft.

Eight C-45Gs and C-45Hs were obtained by the US Army and were all rebuilt C-45s. Serial number 51-11638 is now at the Fort Rucker Aviation Museum. Number 51-11782 had markings for the White Sands Missile Range and 51-11835 had ARADMAC titles, while 52-10859 was named to the Corps of Army Engineers Southwestern Division. An additional four C-45s were used by the Army. One of them was a unique Army C-45 (51-11679), a Volpar Turbo-engine conversion. It was originally an SNB. It is now at the National Museum of Naval Aviation.

All of these C-45s were utilized by the Army as stop-gap aircraft until more modern transports became available. Most were out of the Army inventory by the late 1960s.

This Beech UC-45J (in Kansas City in August 1969) was originally a US Navy SNB-5 (BuNo 51207). The US Army pulled it out of storage at Davis-Monthan AFB for liaison duties. It was returned to MASDC by 1970. It is now flying on the civilian market. *Author*

The US Army painted all of their C-45s in this gloss white (FS16875) over gloss olive drab (FS14087) color scheme. This UC-45J (formally US Navy BuNo 89477) was visiting Kansas City in September 1969. *Author*

The very basic (originally designed in the 1930s) instrument panel in a Beech UC-45F reveals its age. *Beech*

Formally US Navy BuNo 39922, this Beech UC-45J (in Kansas City in September 1970) was operated by the US Army from 1968 to 1972, when it was returned to MASDC. In 1973 it was sold on the civilian market, where it still flies today. *Author*

The Alabama Army National Guard operated this Beech UC-45J (formally US Navy BuNo 89493), here in August 1969, visiting Atlanta, Georgia. It returned to MASDC in 1972, and soon it was on the civilian market, where it still flies today. *Author*

Beech UC-45J (previously US Navy BuNo 51312) was converted to a Volpar tricycle landing gear aircraft. It was one of seven converted for the Army. It was operated by the Anniston Army Depot until 1981, when it was returned to MASDC. It was sold to a civilian in 1984. It crashed in September 2001. The photo is dated fall 1980. *Author*

CHAPTER TWO

T-42A COCHISE

By 1963, the Army wanted an "off-the-shelf" twin-engine aircraft for a multi-engine transition and instrument trainer for fixed-wing aircraft. The U-8 procurement had already ended and U8s were in great demand. Beech suggested their lower-operating-cost Model B55 Baron. Shortly thereafter, the Army placed an initial order for fifty-five T-42A Cochise production aircraft. All production aircraft went to Fort Rucker, Alabama. The first T-42A was delivered on September 2, 1965.

The T-42A was a low-winged, twin-engine aircraft that was smaller than a U-8, but had about the same performance. Accommodations for up to four people, in addition to the pilot, were possible. Normally, though, only two students were flown, along with the instructor

St. Louis, Missouri, was visited by this Beech T-42A (serial number 65-12704) in 1969. The large white ID 04A on the side and the red trim indicate this trainer was stationed at Fort Rucker, Alabama, the US Army's Aviation Training Center. *Author*

pilot. The Cochise was powered by two 260 hp Continental IO-470 engines. They were fitted with dual controls and extensive instrumentation for training. The first T-42A was delivered to Fort Rucker on September 2, 1965. It was slightly different than the civilian version. The T-42A had a longer nose, which increased baggage space by 50%, a 120-lb. gross weight, and new Beechcraft twin-blade constant-speed propellers for improved rate of climb.

Although the T-42 was procured for use as a trainer, high-ranking officers wanted it for their personal aircraft. Thus it was widely used as a light utility aircraft, especially in the Army Reserves and the Army National Guard in its later career. As more U-21s and some C-12s became available, the T-42s were retired.

The USAF acquired at least two T-42As for their needs. Also, one T-42A (65-12797) was converted to a JT-42A for flight testing. Fourteen other countries operated the Beech T-42A around the world. Production lasted until 1972 for the B55 Baron model and totaled 1,956 aircraft, including the military T-42s.

Beech delivered five more T-42As to the US Army for use by the Turkish Army under the Military Assistance Program (MAP). In 1972, a few more T-42s were delivered to the Spanish Air Force.

When the T-42As were being retired by the Army to Davis-Monthan AFB near Tucson, Arizona, they were almost all obtained by civilians. Most are still flying today.

Flying over the countryside, Beech T-42A (serial number 65-12684) displays its standard T-42A color scheme. The T-42A is the military version of the civilian Beech Baron series. All colors are glossy. *Beech*

In the late 1960s, this flight crew member climbs aboard his Beech T-42A for the next flight. The T-42A was a beautiful flying machine and trainer for the Army. Initially Army Aviation used T-42As in twin engine and instrument flight training. *Beech*

Beech T-42A (serial number 65-12687) is ready for the next mission, be it a training flight, a utilitarian flight, or a VIP flight. The T-42A is a small, high-performance, twin-engine trainer, as used by the US Army. *Mark Nankivil*

The flight ramp at Cairns Army Airfield at Fort Rucker, Alabama, in the early 1970s shows numerous Beech T-42As at the ready. *Mark Nankivil*

These two Beech T-42As (in the early 1970s) are camouflaged with no serial numbers or markings. The area behind the pilot's seat is full of "items." They could be two of the five T-42As bought by Turkey. Their actual purpose is a mystery. *Beech*

Beech T-42A (serial number 65-12706) awaits its next training session. Visibility from the cockpit is outstanding because of all the windows. *Beech*

Yellow US Army markings are carried on both wings and both sides of the tail. Later in its military career the T-42A was a coveted utility, liaison, and VIP transport with the US Army. *Beech*

CHAPTER THREE

ARMY SECURITY AGENCY (ASA)

For almost as long as there have been military electronic communications, the US military has been concerned about signal intelligence (SIGINT): the data gathered from the interception, processing, and analysis of electronic communications. The first SIGINT efforts that occurred were during WWI, but it was very haphazard and not organized.

In 1930, the Army organized its first SIGINT unit, called the Signal Intelligence Service (SIS). During WWII, the Army renamed the SIS the Signal Security Agency (SSA). Then, on September 15, 1945, the SSA was renamed the Army Security Agency (ASA). It was commanded by the director of military intelligence for the Army.

In 1945, the ASA was placed under the control of the Armed Forces Security Agency (AFSA). In 1952, the AFSA became the National Security Agency (NSA), which operates under that name today. Because of the need to support combat troops in the Korean War, the ASA expanded by deploying tactical units on a large scale to support the Army in combat. For the first time, the ASA grew to include Army groups and battalions in its force structure. The ASA reported directly to the secretary of defense.

In 1955, the ASA took over all electronic intelligence (ELINT) and electronic warfare functions previously done by the Signal Corps.

All SIGINT missions in Vietnam were controlled by the ASA. In 1976, the ASA changed their name to INSCOM (Intelligence and Security Command). INSCOM exists today and they report directly to the secretary of defense.

CHAPTER FOUR

VIETNAM SERVICE

The first ASA personnel (ninety-two) arrived in Vietnam on May 13, 1961, and set up a post at Tan Son Nhut AFB, just outside Saigon. For cover they were all assigned to the 3rd Radio Research Company. The cover name Radio Research would prevail throughout the Vietnam War, as numerous ASA units also adopted this nomenclature. For the first time a US military unit had been sent to Vietnam as an operational unit. They were not advisers, but a fully functioning field unit.

The ASA people were primarily concerned with locating and monitoring Viet Cong transmitters operating in the south. This was the job of the DF (Direction Finding) specialists. This was why the job was so important and why the program was given such a high priority. The ASA units in the field would locate VC units through DF, identify them by traffic analysis, and notify ARVN units in the area, who would destroy the target and their transmissions. In reality it never worked well in that format. The ASA would find the transmitters, but the ARVN would not follow through.

The ASA troops would mount a PRD-1 receiver or a PRC-10 direction finding unit on a truck or a jeep and by August, they were driving around the area, searching for transmissions in the countryside. On December 22, 1961, SP4 James T. Davis of Livingston, Tennessee (a DF operator), was killed in a Viet Cong ambush on a road outside Saigon. SP4 Davis arguably became the first American soldier to lose his life during the Vietnam War.

The death of Davis brought home to the ASA the dangers of proceeding into the jungle with short-range equipment on a truck to locate VC transmitters, which might be only a few miles away. The answer was an airborne DF platform, so ASA engineers began working on the problem. By March 1962, they had developed the first airborne DF equipment. They put the new equipment in seven de Havilland RU-6A Beavers and called the system SEVEN ROSES. It was here that these ARDF systems began using names like SEVEN ROSES for the new systems.

The data returned from flights was only as accurate as the pilot's navigational skills. Airborne radio direction finding (ARDF) quickly became the single most valuable intelligence resource available to the US military, and remained so throughout the balance of the Vietnam War. In the first four months of operations, aircrews flew 162 missions and identified twenty-three transmitters belonging to approximately sixteen enemy headquarters. The ASA's airborne effort against the VC in the south was so successful that it became MACV's primary source for information for planning ground operations. The signal intelligence that ASA provided quickly surpassed all other intelligence sources in its quality, timeliness, and accuracy. Its ability to find and track movements of NVA and VC units operating in South Vietnam made opposing and destroying them much easier.

Besides the RU-6A Beaver, its bigger brother, the RU-1A Otter, was also tried out as an ARDF. The systems utilized in the Otter were called CAFE GIRL, HAPPY NIGHTS, and LAFFING OTTER.

But the premier ARDF aircraft in Vietnam was the Beech RU-8D Seminole. It had interior capacity, speed, and altitude performance, and it was equipped with Marconi Doppler navigation equipment. The system developed for the RU-8 was called CHECKMATE, with its AN/ARD-15 surveillance equipment. It proved very successful and was extended to the RU-6As. Other systems like WINEBOTTLE and CEFISH PERSON made the RU-8 the true workhorse of the Army's ASA intelligence gathering.

One Army ASA cryptanalyst was Tommy Franks, who later became a general in charge of Central Command in the Middle East.

By the end of 1968, the ASA units in Vietnam numbered eighty aircraft: eighteen RU-6As, thirty-eight RU-8Ds, sixteen RU-21Ds, two U-1As, and six Lockheed RP-2E Neptunes. All were in the 224th Aviation Battalion (RR).

In December 1968, the ASA deployed the first of sixteen RU-21Ds called LAFFING EAGLE. These RU-21 series aircraft increased capability by adding a second SIGINT operator, receivers with a greater frequency range, and an AN/ASN-86 Internal Navigation System. The new system proved very difficult to maintain, but it was efficient. This caused the Army to retire their Lockheed RP-2E Neptunes of the 1st Radio Research Company, the "Crazy Cats." In October 1970, installation of the AN/ARD-23

V-span system on these RU-21Ds was a major coup for ASA ARDF. V-span was the most sophisticated system in the Army's inventory at that time. LAFFING EAGLE soon became the primary source for ARDF intelligence, so other platforms began to stand down.

LAFFING EAGLE was redesignated LEFT JAB in December 1970. This was the first try at 360° direction finding coverage from the aircraft. LEFT JAB was the first system to use digital computers to combine DF and internal navigation information. At the heart of the system was a spinning antenna mounted in a radome under the aircraft. The antenna was extended downward about five feet after takeoff. LEFT JAB flew either a racetrack or a figure 8 search pattern in the mission area. The LEFT JAB program was so highly classified and so electronically advanced in 1971 that the system remained virtually unchanged until the mid-1980s, when an updated version was introduced.

Another system, called LEFT FOOT, combined LAFFING EAGLE's sharper DF feature with the LEFT JAM computer, creating the RU-21E aircraft. Very few LEFT FOOT aircraft flew in Vietnam.

These were all very dangerous missions in Vietnam, since they had to operate over hostile territory to obtain enemy signals. They operated in the "cloak-and-dagger" realm of military intelligence.

CHAPTER FIVE

BEECH L-23/U-8 SEMINOLE

On June 20, 1941, the US Army Air Corps became the US Army Air Force. Disagreements between the Air Corps and ground forces had been simmering for many years. The Air Corps was rapidly developing its concept of strategic air warfare and its ground support program became very weakened. Artillery officers from Fort Sill, Oklahoma (the artillery center), especially bombarded the higher-ups with requests for aerial support. Finally, on June 6, 1942, the War Department officially established organic aviation with the Army Ground Forces (AGF) by overruling complaints of the Army Air Force. Army Aviation was born.

During WWII, Army Aviation fielded many liaison-type aircraft very successfully. When the Korean War started, a huge need developed for staff and VIP flight support. No aircraft existed like that, and it was at the bottom of the list of priorities for the newly formed US Air Force, so the Army started looking around for that type of off-the-shelf and ready-to-go aircraft.

They discovered the Beech Twin Bonanza, which had just recently flown for the first time on November 15, 1949. It fit perfectly into the Army's need for staff and VIP transport. It was a six-seat, all-metal, low-wing cantilever monoplane with flush-riveted skin. On September 20, 1950, Beech began a tour of US military bases for potential military sales.

Beech engineers took a newly developed Beech Bonanza, split it in half, widened it by one foot (thus the one-foot-wide Plexiglas section in the windscreen so the Bonanza windshield could be used), lengthened the airframe, added a rounded nose for the fuselage, and then added a conventional tail. They kept the Bonanza wings to the wing root from the engine nacelle outward, added the twin engines, and then a constant chord wing section to the new fuselage of the Twin Bonanza. This planform is still in use today on the C-12 series.

The Army ordered four "off-the-shelf" Model 50s (as the Twin Bonanza was called by Beech), designated YL-23s, on September 15, 1950. Flight testing began on January 30, 1952, at Fort Sill, Oklahoma, where the artillery center is located. Fort Rucker, Alabama, was not the Army Aviation Center as of this date. Some of the flight testing was also done at Fort Bragg, North Carolina. With flight test evaluation successfully completed, they were painted Olive Drab and shipped off to Korea. Named the Seminole, its high performance and wide landing gear made the L-23 well suited for small field operations. Each held six people, including the pilot.

The prototype Beech Twin Bonanza (N3992N) had its maiden flight on November 15, 1949, in Wichita, Kansas. Its initial price for the civilian market was $30,000. It was yellow with black trim. *Beech*

The Army ordered fifty-five L-23As (all 1952 serial numbers) and forty L-23Bs (all 1953 serial numbers). The first L-23A was delivered to the Army in February 1953. All the A models were delivered in 1953. The only difference between the two was the A model had wooden propellers and the B model had metal propellers. Only the A models saw service in Korea. The first B models were delivered in September 1953, too late to see service in Korea. The last L-23B was delivered in April 1954. All L-23As and L-23Bs were delivered in gloss Olive Drab color.

The Beech earned an excellent reputation in the Army. They were utilized worldwide and were in great demand. They were also used for general utility and liaison missions. In Korea, many USO stars flew in the L-23 to shows. Even South Korean President Syngman Rhee flew in L-23s many times in Korea.

The second Seminole was 52-1802. All four YL-23s were bare metal with minimal markings, and all carried the Army A serial number. The Seminole was exactly the aircraft the Army was looking for. *Beech*

Two Army pilots pose in front of the prototype YL-23, probably at Fort Sill, Oklahoma, home of the Field Artillery School and Field Artillery Training Center. The Artillery Corps of the Army was the instigator for acquiring the Beech L-23 Seminole. *Beech*

The off-the-shelf airplane desired by the US Army was fulfilled by the Beech Twin Bonanza. The first Beech YL-23 was serial number A52-1801. The A in front of the serial number designated the aircraft as an Army aircraft and not an Air Force aircraft. The *A* designation was dropped almost immediately. *Beech*

L-23B serial number 53-6187 had a large *ARMY* painted on the side of the fuselage. Not all early Seminoles had these large letters painted on them. The corrugated tail construction gave the L-23's tail extra strength. This tail was used on all L-23/U-8 series. *Beech*

This L-23A Seminole climbs after takeoff from an airfield in the early 1950s. The wing flaps are lowered for takeoff. The landing gear has not been cycled yet into the up position. *Greater St. Louis Air and Space Museum*

If a US Army three-star general in Korea wanted a bare metal airplane, he got one! Note the red three-star general placard in the window of this early L-23A in Korea. *Beech*

A senior military officer boards a VIP L-23A in Korea. That he is not a general officer is evident because the placard is empty (the placard is on the fuselage just below the vertical antenna on the roof). *Mark Nankivil*

U.S.ARMY
26167

Beech L-23A (serial number 52-6163) was the second production L-23 for the Army. All A and B models were delivered in overall olive drab camouflage (FS34087). This is probably a posed photo. *Beech*

The Army proudly displays its new L-23A (serial number 52-6215) at an air show in 1953. Since there is a curtain in the rear window, this Seminole was probably a VIP transport. The small insignia on the top of the rudder is for the 8th Army. *Beech*

This L-23A Seminole flies formation with another Beech L-23. The pilot is wearing a baseball cap. The craft has a curtain in the rear window, which indicates it is on a VIP mission. *Greater St. Louis Air and Space Museum*

When the Beech L-23 Seminole was being distributed to the US Army, many very senior officers received them. Most VIP L-23s had curtains in the rear windows. *Rainey Bell collection, Greater St. Louis Air and Space Museum*

XL-23C

The XL-23C was actually an L-23B model ordered by the US Air Force on June 20, 1954, for the "Long Tom" project. It was serial number 55-3465 and the only C model built.

Convair was working on a project under the code name "Tom Tom" at the time, involving the use of a Convair GRB-36F and two modified F-84 fighters attached at the wingtips of the B-36. Wing-mounted attachment jaws on each of the F-84s were designed to engage and clamp down on the B-36's wingtips. They were to hold the F-84s in place after in-flight mating was completed. Ground testing of this idea took place at Convair's Fort Worth, Texas, facility. The F-84s were to provide the B-36 with fighter escort. At the same time Convair was testing floating reusable wingtip fuel tanks for the B-36.

These two programs were tested at the same time using the Beech XL-23C, since both programs were so similar in concept. The XL-23C was delivered with US Air Force markings on the tail but in the US Army paint scheme of the time. Later in the flight test program the aircraft changed to US Army markings and color scheme because too many questions about the Air Force markings were being asked. The vast majority of the flight test programs were carried out at Fort Rucker, Alabama.

Both programs were deemed workable and feasible but were never put into operation. It was later converted to a U-8G before retirement.

At Fort Rucker, Alabama, US Air Force, civilian, and Army test pilots flew the only XL-23C (serial number 55-3465), experimenting with outrigger fuel tank equipment. It worked but it was never put to use operationally. *Ray Wilhite*

A close-up of the experimental fuel tank with wheels shows wool tuffs for determining aerodynamic air flow around the tank (it was red and white). Even though the XL-23C was ordered by the US Air Force, after the Air Force was done experimenting, it was given to the US Army. The Army used it for many years as a test aircraft before retiring it. *Ray Wilhite*

L-23D/U-8D

The D model was the main production version of the L-23/U-8 series, and was far and away the most utilized version. Ninety-three of the earlier Model L-23A and L-23B were flown back to Beechcraft in Wichita, Kansas, and rebuilt and reconfigured into the L-23D/U-8D version between September 1957 and August 1959. Two L-23As were no longer flying from the original ninety-five produced. The $1,710,000 contract was awarded on March 25, 1957, to Beech Aircraft by Air Material Command, which orders all Army aircraft from its headquarters at Wright-Patterson Air Force Base, Ohio.

The airframes were zero timed and the engines and propellers replaced. The "new" Seminole was now powered by two Lycoming O-480-1 engines with 340 hp each, and three-bladed metal propellers gave the aircraft a 240 mph high speed and a cruising speed of 228 mph. The engines were super-charged; this model was 40 mph faster than the A or B model. Gross weights were up 1,500 pounds to 7,000 pounds over the A model. The new D model could climb at 1,620 feet per minute and had a service ceiling of 24,800 feet. Its range was 1,650 miles.

The results of the rebuilds of the D model fit perfectly into the US Army's need for staff transport, VIP transport, and other normal liaison duties. Almost all major commands of the Army had their own U-8Ds at one time or another.

At the end of the Vietnam War no U-8s were given to the South Vietnamese because of demand for them by major Army commands worldwide. By the mid-1970s, U-21As returned from Vietnam (Beech U-21As were also not given to the Vietnamese military) and some early C-12s started to become available to major Army commands and major units. These U-8Ds from the major commands

The panel of a Beech U-8D was upgraded from earlier A and B models. Beech used a very logical panel layout on the D model. *Beech*

started to trickle down to the Army National Guard and Reserve units. If a state had a National Guard or Reserve unit in it, the unit probably had a few U-8Ds attached. This was usually done at the state headquarters level, so most U-8Ds were stationed at state capitol airports.

As more C-12s became available the Army started to retire the U-8D fleet. Since the aircraft was built so strong and most still had some life left in them, more than half of all retired Beech U-8Ds eventually found their way into the civilian market. Many are still flying today, even though they are about sixty years old. This is a testament to the basic strong design by Beech and very sound engineering.

Beech L-23D (serial number 57-3085) undergoing minor maintenance in the late 1950s. The open cowlings made for easy ground-level maintenance. *Beech*

PROPELLER

Engine change was fairly easy for the Beech Seminole series, as the engines were at ground level (here in 1958). This Beech is serial number 57-3091. *Beech*

The pilot of this L-23/U-8D (serial number 57-6048) has feathered his left propeller. Luckily, he is right over the airfield in case he has any trouble. *Mark Nankivil*

Flying over the American countryside, Beech Seminole serial number 58-3056 displays a red fuselage vertical stripe in front of the tail. The pilot is wearing his baseball cap. *Mark Nankivil*

Some Beech L-23Ds carried the red (FS11136) and white (FS17875) high-visibility color scheme. This Beech has just arrived, and a 1957 Chevrolet staff car is waiting for the passengers. *Beech*

A close-up view of the U-8 cockpit area shows the one-foot-wide spanner Plexiglas in the center of the windshields. The two outboard windshield Plexiglas panels were designed for the Beech Bonanza. *Beech*

Beech U-8D serial number 57-6042 is on final approach for landing in June 1977. Note the nose landing light is on. *Author*

Beech U-8D serial number 56-3698 shows the newly added weather radar as a small cooling scoop on the upper part of the nose. *Mark Nankivil*

In the late 1950s, two Army officers deplane from Beech L-23D serial number 57-3084 at Seventh Army Operations at Stuttgart, Germany, Army Airfield. Note one Army officer is climbing down the stairs to the ground. *US Army*

These senior Army officers ("scrambled eggs" on the cap visor) have just arrived in their U-8D somewhere in Germany (late 1960s). The two pilots are in flight suits and the staff car is in the foreground. *US Army*

RL-23D/RU-8D

Only seventeen L-23D/U-8Ds were initially converted to RL-23D/RU-8Ds, but they were of vast importance to the SIGINT and COMINT communities of the Army, especially during the Vietnam War. The first two converted L-23Ds were 57-6046 and 58-3060. There were also three new construction RL-23D/RU-8Ds built for a total of twenty for the Army. About thirty more were later converted into RU-8Ds.

Some of these aircraft featured a belly-mounted radar: either an AN/APS-85 in a large pod or an AN/APQ-86 in a long, narrow pod mounted on brackets. This was called a SLAR (Side Looking Airborne Radar) unit. The Grumman OV-1B Mohawk was built to carry this SLAR unit. SLAR was designed to provide all-weather surveillance of the battleground or combat area for intelligence purposes. Some of the RL-23Ds had nose-mounted AN/AVB-50 weather radar. Thus began the marriage of intelligence-gathering equipment and Beech aircraft. The Army Security Agency got involved around this time. In the murky world of classified military intelligence, exact dates, times, data, and information are extremely hard to come by.

ASA's first use of airborne direction finding was in January 1963, in Vietnam. They were using a deHavilland RU-6A Beaver, but the RU-8D offered many advantages over the RU-6A. The Beech had all-weather capability, and it flew higher and faster, plus it could carry more equipment.

By the late 1950s, electronics and avionics were making tremendous advances, especially with the newly developed transistor. This transferred over to electronic monitoring equipment, which now became small enough and good enough to fit into aircraft.

The RU-8D was one of the most flexible and efficient aircraft in the ASA inventory. It could operate in mountainous regions, obtain greater altitude, and offer increased speeds. It quickly became the workhorse of the ASA's airborne direction finding effort in Vietnam, Laos, and Thailand. In 1968, there were forty-four RU-8Ds scattered among four Army Aviation units: the 138th (based at Da Nang), 144th (based at Nha Trang), 146th (based at Tan Son Nhut, near Saigon), and the 156th Aviation (Radio Research, based at Can Tho) Companies.

All were under the 224th Aviation Battalion, along with the 1st Radio Research Company flying Army-marked RP-2E Neptune aircraft out of Nha Trang. All were operated by the ASA. This was a cover for the real operations.

One RU-8D was lost during the Vietnam War: Beech RU-8D (56-1713) crashed on takeoff on December 29, 1967, killing both crew members. The Seminole belonged to the 138th Aviation Company (RR) based in Phu Bai, Vietnam. The North Vietnamese had bounties out for any Radio Research men or aircraft.

The US Navy also operated a Beech U-8D (serial number 58-1339), flown by the Naval Air Engineering Center. The serial number is very small and located on the fuselage under the horizontal stabilizer. *Author*

RL-23D/RU-8D (serial number 58-1360) shows off its underslung SLAR unit and the newly added weather radar on the nose of this Seminole. Note the U-shaped tail skid under the tail to protect the SLAR units from over-rotation on takeoff damage. *Beech*

The weather radar and SLAR unit can be easily seen, but also note the rear windows have been covered over, probably for security reasons. *US Army*

A close-up of the AN/APS-85 SLAR unit shows its cross section is a perfect square with aerodynamic fairings added on both ends. SLAR units were usually mounted on Grumman OV-1 Mohawks. *US Army*

RU-8Ds were prized by the Army. Some RU-8Ds had SLAR units added to them. At the same time the Army added SLAR units they also added an AN/AVB-50 weather radar unit, as seen on the nose of this RU-8D. *US Army*

U.S.ARMY
81348

Beech L-23D/U-8D serial number 58-1348 has been modified to test a PROJECT MICHIGAN AN/UPD-1 airborne radar unit. It affected the aircraft's performance very little, but it was not adopted by the US Army. At least two different aircraft (this one and U-8D 59-2537) were fitted with this unit. *US Army*

The Pink Panther was the logo of the 138th Aviation Company (Radio Research) based at Da Nang AFB, South Vietnam. They flew RU-8Ds until they left Vietnam in March 1973. Barely seen is the white roof of the Seminole. *Robert Pearson*

Beech RU-8D serial number 57-3093 was assigned to the 138th Aviation Company (Radio Research) in Vietnam. The tiger head was on quite a few RU-8Ds in the unit, but the company logo was the Pink Panther. *Don Burnett*

In very small letters on the nose of this RU-8D (serial number 58-1340) is *Kathy*. Kathy was part of the 138th Aviation Company (Radio Research). Most of the RU-8Ds were parked in revetments. *Don Burnett*

CW2 Larry Montague poses on a Beech RU-8D of the 138th Aviation Company (Radio Research). Due to the heat in Vietnam, CW2 Montague always taxied with the windows and door open. *Larry Montague*

Spc. Malcolm McComb poses next to the tiger head art on the cowling of his RU-8D of the 138th Aviation Company (Radio Research). *Malcolm McComb*

Capt. Hardy checks out documents while preflighting an RU-8D for another mission with the 138th Aviation Company (Radio Research). Note the white fuselage top for better cooling in Vietnam. *Steve Weinstein*

In the cockpit of this RU-8D from the 138th Aviation Company (Radio Research) is WO1 Olsen, while in the rear is Spc. Robert Pearson, manning the radio monitoring equipment. Note the white top of the cabin area, which partially reflects the heat of the intense sun in Vietnam. *Robert Pearson*

The flight line of the 138th Aviation Company (Radio Research) was on PSP (pierced steel planking) at Da Nang AFB, South Vietnam. These RU-8Ds are receiving light maintenance from crews. Note the Pink Panther logo of the 138th Aviation Company (Radio Research) on the cowling of the closest RU-8D and the white cabin tops. *Robert Pearson*

An RU-8D is on the ramp awaiting the next mission. The 138th Aviation Company (Radio Research) was based at Da Nang AFB, South Vietnam, for signal monitoring in the northern part of South Vietnam, including the DMZ and I Corps. *Robert Pearson*

Another mission is completed for this RU-8D of the 138th Aviation Company (Radio Research) as the crew disembarks. Note the Pink Panther logo on the cowling. *Robert Pearson*

In preparation for the next mission, this RU-8D is being refueled on the ramp of the 138th Aviation Company (Radio Research) at Da Nang AFB, South Vietnam. Most revetment walls were built out of empty bomb shipping containers and filled with dirt or sand. *Robert Pearson*

Note the top of the cabin is painted white for better cooling in tropical Vietnam. This RU-8D of the 138th Aviation Company (Radio Research) waits in line for takeoff from Da Nang AFB. *Robert Pearson*

For some unknown reason, the 138th Aviation Company operated this RU-8D (serial number 58-11342) in bare metal—the only bare metal U-8 to operate in Vietnam. *Tom Baca*

Beech RU-8D serial number 57-6082 returns to Da Nang AFB after another mission for the 138th Aviation Company (Radio Research). Note the Pink Panther on the cowling, the white top of the fuselage cabin, and the U-shaped tail skid under the tail so the SLAR unit will not drag on landing or takeoff. *Robert Pearson*

The open window of this RU-8D of the 146th Aviation Company (Radio Research) reveals some of the radio monitoring equipment behind the pilot's seat. *US Army*

Red and green prop spinners adorn the RU-8D belonging to the 138th Aviation Company (Radio Research). The colors matched the wingtip navigation lights. The 138th was based at Da Nang AFB, South Vietnam. Light maintenance is being performed on the engine. *Lansing Williams*

The flight line of the 146th Aviation Company (Radio Research) at Tan Son Nhut AFB, South Vietnam, in November 1966, shows some of their fleet of RU-8Ds. *Author*

L-23E/U-8E

The Army wanted a few extra-range Seminoles for various reasons, so six were ordered and delivered in 1956. The changes included different engines for better fuel economy. The E model had two Lycoming GO-480-G2D6 engines of 295 hp each. It had fuel tanks of 180 US gallons, plus two optional 23 US gallon auxiliary tanks. Two of these E models were converted to U-8G models (56-4041 and 56-4044).

A single commercial Twin Bonanza NU-8E (serial number 66-15360) was acquired for "special electronic testing." It was probably a reclaimed drug aircraft. The Army occasionally used this type of aircraft.

Not all reclaimed drug aircraft were given valid military serial numbers; some were given bogus registrations and serial numbers. Some were utilized in classified or "nonexistent" operations.

Beech U-8F serial number 60-3453 (see opposite) was the Army's version of the civilian Beech Queen Air. It had the same tail unit, wings, engines, and landing gear of the D model but a completely new fuselage. *US Army*

One of six L-23Es (shown new in 1956) ordered by the Army. The L-23E had no external differences from the L-23D series. It had more fuel tanks in the wings and slightly different engines for a longer range. *Mark Nankivil*

L-23F/U-8F

The F model was a dramatic upgrade to the Seminole series of aircraft for the Army. The fuselage was completely redesigned for larger seating capacity and cargo volume. It was based on the commercial Queen Air Beechcraft. In 1958, the Army ordered three off-the-shelf examples of the Queen Air for evaluation as the L-23F. Using the L-23D's wings, engines, and tail group, the Model 65—as Beech called the Queen Air—featured an all-new fuselage that was lengthened and widened, with aisle-type seating for six passengers and two pilots. This new fuselage was the basis for all future U-21 series and C-12 series airframes.

In a series of contracts between 1959 and 1963, the Army bought a further seventy-six Model 65s as U-8Fs. Three ex-civilian model 65 Queen Airs were added to the Army inventory as U-8Fs: one in 1966, and two more in 1981. These were confiscated from drug smugglers. U-8Fs formed the backbone of the MACV VIP and staff transports in Vietnam until the U-21As became available. The U-8Fs were then distributed to the Reserves and the National Guard, and finally withdrawn from service in the early 1990s.

An RU-8F ARDF operated in Vietnam for a short time with the same sensor array as the RU-8D.

The NU-8F designation was used by one single modified U-8F in 1964 (serial number 63-12903); it was delivered to Fort Rucker, Alabama, in March 1964. This aircraft was the prototype of the turbine-powered King Air series, which evolved into the U-21 series and the C-12 series. It was powered by two 500hp Pratt & Whitney PT-6A-6 turboprop engines.

Beech U-8F serial number 60-3453 flies over the Western United States in the early 1970s. The U-8F was based on the civilian Beech Queen Air model. *Beech*

The Army Beeches were very rugged and were able to operate from grass airstrips. Beech U-8F serial number 62-3871 proves it here. *Beech*

The interior of the Beech U-8F approaches commercial airline quality, as shown in this 1960 view of the instrument panel. Note the curtains and fresh air vents. *Beech*

A female pilot climbs down the stairs of a Beech U-8F in the 1980s. Now there are numerous female pilots in the Army. *US Army*

The L-23F/U-8F had a much bigger fuselage, which was wider, longer, and taller than the D model, fulfilling the Army's need for a larger aircraft. This Seminole is taxiing out for another mission from a Western United States airfield. *US Army*

The first production L-23F/U-8F was serial number 58-1354. It was vigorously tested at Fort Rucker, Alabama, then authorized for Army use after passing. *Beech*

Later the first production U-8F was transferred to the US Army Transportation Center at Fort Eustis, Virginia. By May 1966, it had a red rudder and a red fuselage stripe. *Author*

The Beech U-8F was utilized by MACV Flight Section based at Tan Son Nhut AFB near Saigon, South Vietnam. MACV (Military Assistance Command Vietnam) had at least a dozen or so U-8Fs like 62-3864, here in February 1967. *Author*

This Beech U-8F (serial number 60-3455) at an air show in fall 1973 belonged to the Army Air Defense Command. *Author*

U-8G

The U-8G designation was assigned after the 1962 redesignations of military aircraft. Eleven U-8Ds were rebuilt with new Lycoming 340 hp O-480-CSC6 engines, easier passenger seating, and upgraded avionics.

In 1962, all existing aircraft in the L-23 series received the new designation U-8, keeping the same letter model numbers.

XL-23C (serial number 55-3465) was the test aircraft for the wing extension experiments. After the tests were completed the aircraft was redesignated a U-8G. Here it is entering storage at Davis-Monthan AFB near Tucson, Arizona. *Author*

The New Jersey Army National Guard operated this Beech U-8F in the late 1970s and early 1980s. It was stationed at the state capital, Trenton, New Jersey. The serial number is 62-3851. *Author*

A MACV Flight Detachment Beech U-8F (serial number 62-3867) awaits passengers on the ramp at Tan Son Nhut AFB near Saigon, South Vietnam, in February 1967. MACV U-8Fs were parked next to the RU-8Ds of the 146th Aviation Company (Radio Research) and across the ramp from Air America and the defoliant C-123s of Operation Ranch Hand, which sprayed Agent Orange over South Vietnam. *Author*

CHAPTER SIX

BEECH U-21UTE

U-21A

The Army was quite pleased with the NU-8F. In October 1966, the Army ordered the unpressurized version and called it the U-21A. This was the beginning of a long and varied career for this type.

The new U-21A could accommodate up to ten troops, plus a flight crew of two pilots. It could be quickly adapted for air evacuation ambulance or cargo-carrying duties. Beech added a forward-hinged cargo door, giving an opening of 4 ft. 5 1/2 in. × 4 ft. 31/2 in. It could carry 3,000 lb. of cargo and accommodate up to ten combat troops along with the crew of two.

It was powered by two Pratt & Whitney PT-6A-20 turboprops with 550 hp each. The propellers were three-bladed, reversible, constant-speed Hartzell HC-B3TN-3/T10173s.

The airframe of the U-21A was similar to that of the Beech Model 65-B80; only the forward-hinged cargo door was different. All-weather operation was made possible by a full set of electronics, navigational aids, and de-icing equipment. In March 1967, only four months after design had started, the prototype made its initial flight.

The Army ordered 40 for 1966 and 78 for 1967, making a total of 118 ordered. Eventually 141 would be acquired. The Army took delivery of the first U-21A on May 16, 1967. The first U-21As began reaching units in Vietnam in fall 1967; they were distributed to various major commands. Two aircraft (66-18004 and 67-18096) were loaned to the US Navy.

The wings, tail, and landing gear were all from the King Air series of Beech aircraft, while the fuselage came from the Queen Air series. Nearly one-quarter of the A model fleet was eventually converted for a variety of electronic intelligence missions. At least thirty were modified as special electronic mission aircraft (SEMA).

The prototype of all turbine-powered U-21s and C-12s for the military and of all King Airs for the civilian market was NU-8F, the turbine-powered version of the U-8F (serial number 63-12902). It had a red stripe on the fuselage and a partial red tail. The turbine-powered Beech has now been in production for over fifty years. More than 6,000 have been produced for the military and civilian markets. *Beech*

At least eighteen Beech U-21A Utes await delivery to the US Army at Beech's Wichita, Kansas, plant. Note all of the civilian Beeches also awaiting delivery. Almost all of the early production U-21As were assigned to Vietnam. *Beech*

A full flight line of newly manufactured Beech U-21As at the Beech factory in Wichita, Kansas. Army personnel are inspecting one of the new Utes. *Beech*

The first production Beech U-21A (serial number 66-18000) demonstrates the loading of cargo through its large fuselage doors. *Beech*

A newly delivered Beech U-21A Ute to Vietnam awaits its unit assignment and delivery at Tan Son Nhut AFB, South Vietnam, in September 1967. *Author*

This Beech U-21A is freshly delivered to Tan Son Nhut AFB, South Vietnam. The U-21As were in great demand by various high commands and units in Vietnam. *Author*

Beech 21A serial number 66-18029 was assigned to the Aviation Section of the 1st Signal Brigade at Tan Son Nhut AFB near Saigon, Vietnam, in September 1967. The author flew two tours of duty with this unit in Vietnam. This Ute was not converted to an electronic aircraft but kept as a utility aircraft. *Author*

Beech U-21A serial number 66-18004 was loaned to the US Naval Test Pilots School at Patuxent River Naval Warfare Center (Pax River), Maryland. Here it is at NAS Whiting Field on October 21, 1994. *Henk Schnitemaker*

The US Naval Test Pilots School's titles and crest are carried on both sides of the U-21. The Ute was aircraft number 37 at the school. *Henk Schnitemaker*

After the Vietnam War ended, all remaining Beech U-21As were returned to the States. None were given to the Vietnamese because of demand by major units of the US Army. U-21A serial number 66-18008 was assigned to the USAAEFA (US Army Aviation Engineering Flight Activity). It is shown here in Duluth, Minnesota, conducting icing tests on other aircraft. The U-21 is the spray aircraft. The silver tanks above the cockpit spray water into the air where the test aircraft will fly. *Author*

Beech U-21A serial number 67-18099 was operated by the Minnesota Army National Guard and was stationed in St. Paul, Minnesota, the capital of Minnesota and the state headquarters of the National Guard. *Author*

Three Beech U-21As pose in flight over the Kansas prairies. The upper U-21 has the standard Army olive drab color scheme, the center U-21 has the high-visibility red-and-white color scheme, and the U-21 in the foreground has a bare metal with red tail color scheme. The bare metal scheme was very rare. *Beech*

This factory fresh Beech U-21A (serial number 66-0035) arrived at Tan Son Nhut AFB, Saigon, Vietnam, in September 1967. It was then delivered to its unit or command for military service. *Author*

The First United States Army Command operated this Beech U-21A (serial number 68-18047). A full bird colonel's placard is in the rear window. Only colonels (O-6) and above in rank had red placards carried on aircraft. *Author*

Fort Polk, Louisiana, was the operator of U-21A serial number 67-18060 in the 1980s. U-21s were very flexible in their assigned missions. Most U-21s were maintained in pristine condition. *Author*

Pentagon liaison utility support was provided by this U-21A with Military District of Washington (DC) markings and also other aircraft. If a Pentagon general officer needs a flight, he or she gets a flight. *Author*

When not on water-spraying icing duties in Duluth, Minnesota, in the wintertime, U-21A serial number 66-18008 performs other engineering flight test duties (USAAEFA stands for United States Army Aviation Engineering Flight Activity). *Author*

U-21A Utes were powered by a pair of Pratt & Whitney of Canada PT-6A-20 turboprop engines producing 550 hp. This was more than adequate for the A model, giving great performance. *Author*

Another factory fresh Beech U-21A has just arrived at Tan Son Nhut AFB and is awaiting assignment to its unit or command in September 1967. *Author*

The Armor Center at Fort Knox, Kentucky, operated this U-21A. The American flag is proudly displayed on the tail. Most major Army commands had at least one Beech U-21A for liaison duties. The American flag means the aircraft has gone overseas. *Author*

Yuma Proving Grounds operated this Beech U-21A Ute (serial number 66-18036) for support of various projects. Most U-21As wore this color scheme during their entire careers, the exception being that most Vietnam Utes were overall olive drab. *Author*

EU-21A

The first electronic conversion of a U-21A was the EU-21A. At least five (66-18000—the first production aircraft—66-18013, 66-18027, 67-18055, and 67-18058) were modified for use as airborne radio relay platforms. They carried no special antennas, so they looked like normal U-21As. At least one (66-18027) was assigned to the 1st Signal Brigade, Aviation Section, the unit the author flew with while in Vietnam.

The electronic equipment was later removed, and the aircraft were all reverted to normal U-21As.

EU-21A serial number 66-18027 of the 1st Signal Brigade, Aviation Section, Vietnam, carried its name, Black Sheep, on the nose. The soldier is conducting minor maintenance on the right engine. *Author*

The first electronic Beech U-21A was 66-18027 of the Aviation Section of the 1st Signal Brigade. Called an EU-21A, the top half of the fuselage was painted white for cooling in the tropics of Vietnam. All 1st Signal Brigade aircraft carried a fluorescent orange strip on the rudder tips. SP/5 Eugene C. Allen is working on the nose wheel in January 1968. *Author*

GU-21A

Two airframes were eventually used for ground instruction (66-18006 and 66-18012).

JU-21A

Three U-21As were converted to JU-21As (66-18002, 66-18008, and 67-18060). One of them (66-18008) was modified for use as an aerial test bed for the AN/ARQ-38 LEFT JAB VHF direction finding SIGINT system. It was developed by the Army's Electronic Warfare Laboratory (EWL) at Fort Monmouth, New Jersey. All three were LEFT JAB equipped.

The most visible modification was the retractable, oval-shaped pod on the lower fuselage. The pod would be lowered about five feet during flight for better signal reception. The rest of the time it stayed up next to the belly of the aircraft.

After returning from Vietnam, the aircraft were assigned to the Army Reserve and later reverted to a normal U-21A configuration.

The only ASA aircraft shot down in Vietnam was JU-21A LEFT JAB (serial number 67-18065), from the 138th Aviation Company, based in Phu Bai. It was lost on March 4, 1971. Call sign Vanguard 216 was on a top secret mission to supposedly collect intelligence on surface-to-air missile sites either in the DMZ or north of the DMZ. Its mission is *still* classified. An all-out effort was made to locate the crash because of the highly classified equipment onboard. It was never found, but the intelligence equipment onboard was never exploited, so the North Vietnamese never found the crash site either.

Three Beech U-21As were converted into JU-21As with LEFT JAB sensor systems. In flight the sensor was lowered about five feet for better signal reception. They were very effective at detecting enemy signal traffic. *US Army*

The LEFT JAB sensor is easily seen under the fuselage of this JU-21A. This JU-21A (call sign was Vanguard 216) was shot down on March 4, 1971. *Lee Hendley*

The JU-21A had a bubble side cockpit window for better downward visibility. In the cockpit is Capt. Mike Marker, who was later killed when his LEFT JAB JU-21A was shot down over North Vietnam on March 4, 1971. *Jim Methvin*

Two of the three LEFT JAB JU-21As are flying in formation with other U-21As. LEFT JAB aircraft never operated in pairs in Vietnam, always flying missions alone. *US Army*

RU-21A

Four U-21As (67-18112 through 67-18115) were converted to countermeasure jamming sets using AN/ULQ-11 equipment. This airborne intercept, direction finding, and jamming system used the program name CRAZY DOG and later CEFIRM LEADER. This system would also be carried by three other variants of the U-21, and they were also equipped with AN/ARD-22 radio DF equipment.

They had four flat-bladed antennas installed along the cabin roof and vertical, long, narrow antennas projecting upward and downward near the wingtips. Later the antennas were replaced by wingtip pods, which looked like fuel tanks but were not. There were also at least three flat-bladed antennas on the belly of the aircraft.

The Army flew this model from 1972 to 1993, including in Operation Desert Storm. RU-21A serial number 67-18112 was lost in a ditching off the coast of Greece.

Due to congressional rules the three RU-21As were retired and stored at Davis-Monthan AFB, then put up for sale, but the Army put an astronomical price on them so no one would want to acquire them. From the "fittings and modifications" still on the aircraft, someone might be able to determine the equipment that was mounted in them.

The U-21 series had an updated cockpit panel display. This was before "glass cockpits" evolved. *Beech*

The first RU-21A was 67-18112. It was a test bed aircraft monitored by very senior general Army officers, so the olive drab paint was stripped and the bare metal was highly polished. *Gerald Belzer collection via Mark Nankivil*

RU-21A serial number 67-18115 was one of four aircraft operating the CRAZY DOG system, which developed into the CEFIRM LEADER system and later into the CRAZY HORSE system. The RU-21As retired in 1993, when they were replaced by much updated versions of these systems in C-12 aircraft. *Author*

Beech RU-21A serial number 67-18113 was a CEFIRM LEADER sensor system aircraft. It was retired in 1993. The system later became the CRAZY HORSE system. The wingtips hold sensors and are not fuel tanks. *Robert Burgess collection via Mark Nankivil*

RU-21A serial number 67-18114 belonged to the 138th Radio Research Company of the 224th Military Intelligence Battalion based in Germany. During the first Iraqi War in 1991, the Ute carried nose art showing "From the Us." *A. Rodriquez*

RU-21B

Three RU-21Bs were built (67-18077, 66-18087, and 67-18093). They were all delivered to the 138th Aviation Company (RR) in Phu Bai, Vietnam. Due to the additional weight of the electronic intelligence equipment onboard, these were built with the Pratt & Whitney PT-6A-29 engines with 620 hp each. The RU-21B also had heavier landing gear struts and dual wheels on the main gear. It did not have the slender wingtip antennas of the RU-21A.

After the Vietnam War the three were based near Fort Bliss, Texas. These aircraft were equipped with the AN/ALR-32 electronic countermeasure receiving sets and formed the intercept and collection components of the AN/ULQ-11 countermeasure jamming set called CEFIRM LEADER.

All RU-21Bs were scrapped in 1993 under mysterious conditions at Opa Locka Airport in Florida.

RU-21C

Two RU-21Cs were built (67-18085 and 67-18089). They were very similar to the RU-21B, and were also assigned to the 138th Aviation Company (RR) in Phu Bai, Vietnam, in 1967. They had a slightly different antenna array than the B model.

These aircraft were equipped with the AN/ALT-29 countermeasure transmitting set and served as the jamming component for the AN/ULQ-11 countermeasure jamming set called CEFIRM LEADER. They also had stronger dual wheel main landing gear like the B model and the same engines as the B model. After their Vietnam service they were operated by USAECOM, and later in Honduras in the early 1980s during the civil war in El Salvador. Plus they were deployed to Egypt for the Bright Star 85 exercises. In addition, they had many deployments to NAS Key West, Florida, and throughout other Caribbean locations at the behest of the national intelligence services, as well as counter-narcotic missions directed by the US Army.

All RU-21As, Bs, and Cs complemented each other.

"Sportsman" was displayed on the nose of RU-21B serial number 67-18087 of the 138th Radio Research Company of the 224th Military Intelligence Battalion based in Germany, here seen during the Iraqi War in 1991. *A. Rodriquez*

RU-21C serial number 67-18085 of the 138th Radio Research Company, 224th Military Intelligence Battalion. While in Europe this unit flew in support of USAECOM (United States Army European Command). The nose art says "From Rags To Riches." *A. Rodriquez*

RU-21D

The development of the RU-21D was a direct result of the success of the RU-21A, B, and C models in Vietnam. Since there was a greater need for more sophisticated electronic warfare platforms, the Army ordered thirty-four of this variant, but only eighteen were built (67-18104 through 67-18111 and 67-18119 through 67-18128). The other sixteen became RU-21Es. They had a modified cockpit layout and upgraded avionics.

The RU-21D used the airborne radio direction finding platform AN/ARD-23 called LAFFING EAGLE, but LAFFING EAGLE was never fielded and these aircraft were further modified to Guardrail configurations.

Like the C models, they were powered by two Pratt & Whitney PT-6A-28 engines. At least seven of the RU-21D were deconfigured after the Army did not adopt the system and converted to plain U-21Ds. Three RU-21Ds were converted to RU-21Hs. RU-21D 67-18125 was converted to a JRU-21D.

An RU-21D lands at Quang Tri, South Vietnam, after completion of another mission in 1971. *Robert Brakenhoff*

In 1971, Beech RU-21D serial number 67-18105 is in a hangar in Quang Tri, South Vietnam. The Pink Panther on the cowling shows it belongs to the 138th Aviation Company (Radio Research). On the nose is painted "Humpin' Mutha." *Robert Brakenhoff*

RU-21D serial number 67-18093 had covered fuselage windows, which blocked the view of the electronic sensor equipment inside. *Author*

This RU-21D (serial number 67-18119) belonged to the 146th Aviation Company (Radio Research), stationed at Tan Son Nhut AFB, Saigon, Vietnam. *A 146th RRCo member*

RU-21D serial number 67-18105 rests at its revetment at Da Nang AFB, South Vietnam, in 1972. It belonged to the 138th Aviation Company (Radio Research). *Clark Mullins*

On April 21, 1983, this RU-21D (serial number 67-18113) was visiting an air show. Continuing to the present, most RU-21s have the same overall gray color (FS36231). *Author*

This U-21D (serial number 67-18108) belongs to the US Army Reserve Command. Note the major general's two-star red placard in the rear window. *Author*

RU-21D serial number 67-18112 has covered-up windows, which was common on the RU-21 series. People often mistake the wingtip sensors for fuel tanks. *Author*

RU-21E

The RU-21E was from the order for RU-21Ds (sixteen were built, serial numbers 70-15875 to 70-15890). These aircraft were actually built to A model specifications. They were intended from the start to be electronic reconnaissance aircraft and were equipped with an advanced AN/ARD-26 RDF system called LEFT FOOT. Although the system was more advanced than LAFFING EAGLE, it was never adopted by the Army.

All sixteen of these models were later converted to the Guardrail system and redesignated RU-21Hs. These E models were externally identical to the D model.

Beech RU-21E serial number 70-15880 flies over the American countryside. The E model has six pairs of vertical antenna sensors. *Beech*

This RU-21E (serial number 70-15882) carried the GUARDRAIL IV sensor system onboard in this 1974 photograph of it flying over the Western United States. It was redesignated an RU-21H when converted to the standard GUARDRAIL system. *Beech*

Sixteen RU-21Es were built; serial number 70-15877 was the third. Sensor antennas were also now on the horizontal stabilizer. *Mark Nankivil*

Serial number 70-15898 was one of three RU-21Gs. In 1971, they were outfitted with the GUARDRAIL I airborne electronic sensor equipment. It carries some very unique antenna arrays. *Beech*

This Ute (serial number 70-15880) is factory fresh before the airborne electronic sensor equipment is added. Externally, it is identical to the U-21A series. *Beech*

U-21F

Five F models (70-15908 through 70-15912) were ordered "off-the-shelf" for general utility transport work. These were the first pressurized aircraft for the Army. They had round windows instead of unpressurized square windows. Pratt & Whitney PT-6A-28 engines of 680 hp each powered the F model using four-bladed propellers. All five carried plush civilian interiors that could carry up to thirteen passengers. They entered the Army inventory in 1971.

The US Navy used a few of these aircraft at the Naval Test Pilots School (NTPS) in the late 1990s. The Army obtained a sixth F model, which was a confiscated drug smuggling aircraft (serial number 90-0060).

The U-21F was the first pressurized aircraft for the US Army. They were built with round windows instead of unpressurized square windows. Note the dual-wheeled main landing gear due to the extra weight of the aircraft and the electronic equipment on board. This Ute was assigned to the Military District of Washington (DC)—aka the Pentagon—in October 1982. *Author*

Beech U-21F serial number 70-15909 (on June 10, 1977) was assigned to the Military District of Washington (DC)—the Pentagon. Barely seen in the rear window is a placard for a four-star general. *Author*

U-21G

These were the final seventeen Utes built new for the Army (70-15891 through 70-15907). They were identical to the U-21A, but had a cockpit reconfiguration and avionics. Nine were eventually converted to SEMA aircraft. Since they were unpressurized they had square windows.

A new Beech U-21G (serial number 70-15905) assigned to USAEUR (United States Army Europe), as seen by the badge on the cowling. It is parked at Heidelberg Airfield in Germany, home of the 207th Aviation Company. The 207th converted to C-12s in 1978. *US Army*

Beech U-21G serial number 70-15896 was in transit in Prestwick, Scotland, on February 21, 1976. It is painted in high-visibility markings, showing a red-and-white color scheme. *Paul Thallon*

Serial number 70-15904 was a U-21G assigned to the Fifth United States Army. The U-21G was the last of the U-21 series built for the US Army. *Author*

RU-21G

Three U-21Gs were converted to RU-21Gs (70-15893, 70-15898, and 70-15899). They were outfitted with an airborne communication intelligence system called Guardrail I, which was developed by ESL in 1971.

Guardrail I was unlike other airborne systems used by the Army. It was operated remotely from a ground-based integrated processing facility, so the only flight crew were the two pilots. It had multiple antenna arrays on the fuselage and large sensor pods on the wingtips that look like fuel tanks. All three RU-21Gs were converted to RU-21Hs.

RU-21G serial number 70-15898 carries the GUARDRAIL V airborne electronic sensor system in 1978. *Beech*

The fuselage windows are covered over on this RU-21H (serial number 70-15879) on April 6, 1991. Note the bat emblem on the tail. The RWAH sensor on the nose cone (for antiaircraft missile warnings) and the antennas covered by the dorsal fin are some details noted. *Manfred Faber*

Beech RU-21H serial number 70-15883 was originally an RU-21E. It became an H model when it was converted to the GUARDRAIL V airborne electronic sensor equipment. *Author*

RU-21H serial number 70-15884 visits NAS Moffett Field in October 1980 during an air show. They attract attention at air shows due to their uniqueness. *Author*

Beech NU-21H serial number 70-15888 was operated by the US Army Missile Command (here in July 1986). As a test aircraft, this UTE externally mounted missiles for aerodynamic data on the missiles. Note the wool tufts attached to the bottom rear fuselage for monitoring airflow disruption around the missile. *Author*

This RU-21 carried the name "Sweet Cream Lady" on the nose. It was operated by the 138th Aviation Company (Radio Research), based at Da Nang AFB, South Vietnam. *Ron Hull*

Open cargo doors reveal the massive electronic sensor equipment in this Ute. This RU-21 belonged to the 333rd Electronic Warfare Aviation Company of the 2nd Military Intelligence Battalion, based at Ramstein AFB, Germany, supporting the 7th Army in Europe. *Jeff Dawson*

U-21H

After the replacement of RU-21Hs by more modern C-12 equipment, the Army wanted to modify thirty-six examples of the H model to U-21H standards by stripping them all back to the normal utility version. About twenty-three had been converted when the US Air Force transferred their C-12F fleet to the Army, making the U-21 conversion unnecessary. The balance of the unconverted U-21s were placed in storage at Davis-Monthan AFB.

JU-21H

Two RU-21E (70-15877 and 70-15888) LEFT FOOT aircraft were converted to JU-21Hs. They were stripped of their electronic equipment and assigned to the US Army Aviation Technical Test Center at Fort Rucker, Alabama. These were the last U-21s in service with the US Army and were retired on January 4, 2000.

RU-21H

Starting during 1976, twenty-one RU-21Ds, RU-21Es, and RU-21Gs were converted to RU-21Hs with the AN/ARD-9 Guardrail V system. Guardrail was an automatic, remotely controlled SIGINT/DF equipment program capable of detecting, locating, classifying, and recording enemy signal emissions. The RU-21H could provide friendly forces with hard information about precise positions of enemy forces and their intentions. Some aircraft also included jamming equipment. Guardrail was such an important system that it made it almost impossible for an enemy to communicate by radio or other electronic signals.

All H models had the two large pods on the wingtips. The RU-21H had AN/ALQ-36 and ALQ-44 radar warning equipment and was also equipped with an M-130 chaff/flare system. The H model worked so well it was the longest lasting U-21 Guardrail version. The H models were retired in 1994, when more modern C-12s took over.

RU-21J

To avoid confusion between the letter *I* and the number *1*, there was no I model of the U-21 series. In 1971, the Army bought three off-the-shelf Beech Model 200 King Airs (serial numbers 71-21058 through 71-21060) and gave them the RU-21J designation. They were meant to be the airborne platform for the new CEFTY LANCER AN/USQ-71 system. These aircraft were powered by two Pratt & Whitney PT-6A-41 850 hp engines and had the new T tail on a stretched, pressurized fuselage. The RU-21J also had a revised wing with a larger span, increased fuel capacity, and more pressurization for operating at higher ceiling altitudes and a longer range.

The CEFTY LANCER system was not adopted into Army service, so these aircraft were reconfigured as VIP transports. Since these aircraft were actually C-12s, they were redesignated C-12Ls. They were retired in 1997.

In Vietnam the 138th Aviation Company (Radio Research) used the Pink Panther as their company logo. Spc. Ron Sandsrtom also added the shark mouth to his RU-21. *Don Burnett*

SP/5 Clark Mullins poses on the stairway of his RU-21 of the 138th Aviation Company (Radio Research) in July 1972. Part of the airborne sensor equipment can be seen behind Clark. *Clark Mullins*

The Beech RU-21J (here the number two aircraft, serial number 71-21059, on April 28, 2005) was actually the first of the C-12 series bought by the US Army. It was built for the CEFLY LANCER airborne platform. Only three were bought. *Beech*

The interior of the RU-21 series was relatively cramped for the system operator. The sensor equipment took up lots of space in these early 1970s systems. *Clark Mullins*

CHAPTER SEVEN

BEECH VC-6A

VC-6A

The VC-6A was a transition from the U-21 series to the C-12 series. There were only two built and operated by the US military. They are basically just a standard U-21A but pressurized. They were Model 65-A90.

The first one was 66-7943. It was used by President Lyndon Johnson between Bergstrom AFB, near Austin, Texas, and the Johnson family ranch near Johnson City, Texas. When LBJ was onboard, the aircraft used the call sign Air Force One. The aircraft is now on display with other presidential aircraft at the National Museum of the United States Air Force at Wright-Patterson AFB, Dayton, Ohio.

The other VC-6A was serial number 66-15361. It was stationed at Redstone Army Arsenal, where rockets and missiles were being developed for the military and NASA. It was the personal aircraft of Dr. Wernher von Braun and was frequently flown to and from White Sands Proving Grounds in New Mexico.

After Dr. von Braun died, the aircraft was assigned to the Dugway Proving Grounds in Utah as a test aircraft. It was retired in 1994, and is now on display at the White Sands Missile Range.

The first pressurized U-21A was serial number 66-7943, and it was designated VC-6A. It was delivered to the US Air Force and assigned to the 1254th Special Air Missions Squadron of the 89th Military Airlift Wing. It was based at Andrews AFB. It was frequently Air Force One when used by President Johnson. *Dave Ostrowski*

The VC-6A was basically used for flying President Johnson to his ranch in Texas from a nearby Air Force base. This aircraft was the basis for the C-12 series. *Greater St. Louis Air and Space Museum*

The second of two VC-6As was serial number 66-15361, which was originally NU-8F. It was delivered to the Redstone Army Arsenal in July 1966. It was for transporting Dr. Wernher von Braun and his missile engineers to and from White Sands Missile Range for the Army. It was retired in 1984 to the White Sands Missile Range Museum (as shown). *Author*

CHAPTER EIGHT

BEECH C-12 HURON

C-12A

Beech project studies led to the introduction of the Beech Super King Air B200 in mid-1969. The aircraft's most significant feature was its large T tail. The new tail assembly produced better efficiency of the rudder and elevator since they were in the clean, undisturbed airstream. This also reduced aerodynamic loads. The new model first flew on October 27, 1972.

The Beech 200 Super King Air had an increased wingspan using extended wingtips, a new T tail, additional fuel capacity, increased cabin pressurization, and a higher weight. It was bigger, faster, and more capable than the U-21s in service with the Army.

The C-12A is actually the RU-21J's nonelectronic version. It was so different from the U-21 series that it was redesignated a C-12A Huron. It was powered by two Pratt & Whitney PT-6A-38 engines of 750 hp with three-bladed props.

The US Air Force took delivery of their first C-12A on July 23, 1975. The Army took delivery of their first C-12As at Fort Monroe, Virginia. Two of the C-12As were utilized by US Customs (73-22265 and 73-33366). The Army took delivery of sixty C-12As over a four-year serial number time span (1973–1977). The US Air Force also bought thirty of the same aircraft, and their serial numbers are intermixed with the Army's serial numbers. The C-12 series was utilized by all four military branches and by about thirty foreign countries, making it one of the most exported military aircraft behind the Lockheed C-130.

These models were intended to replace earlier U-21As for staff support and VIP flights. They were all fitted with a military cockpit, weather radar, and an autopilot. The commercial version could hold thirteen passengers, but the military C-12A was designed to have only eight plush seats.

The B model was a US Navy purchase designated UC-12B. In 1978, the Navy bought the first of seventy-eight C-12s for use as personnel and utility transports. The Navy also converted some of their versions to NC-12Bs and TC-12Bs.

The Army did not have any B model C-12s.

The C-21A number one production Huron was serial number 73-22250. The C-12 was based on the civilian Beech King Air 200 series. The 6,000th King Air came off the Beech production line in December 2004. The typical price is around $3 million, which is cheap for an advanced military aircraft. *Beech*

UNITED STATES ARMY

The Beech C-12A replaced the U-21 as a VIP, liaison, and utility aircraft for the US Army. It was longer, was faster, and flew higher than the U-21, although it was a similar aircraft. The United States Army operated this C-12A at the time on May 27, 1982. *Author*

C-12C

The next Army purchase of the C-12 series was the C-12C. The Army ordered fourteen (78-23126 through 78-23139). They were based on the Beech Model A200. The C-12C was identical to the C-12A, but had Pratt & Whitney PT-6A-41 engines of 850 hp each. All surviving C-12As were eventually brought up to C-12C standards. In 1989, five C models were "civilianized" for use in covert operations. Also, some drug smuggling aircraft might have been utilized here.

The Sixth United States Army operates this C-12C (serial number 73-22267). The Sixth United States Army (US Army South) is based at Fort Sam Houston, near San Antonio, Texas. *Author*

C-12C serial number 73-22263 belonged to the USA STRATCOM (United States Army Strategic Communications), a part of the Signal Corps. This March 1981 photograph was taken at a Western United States airbase. *Author*

The US Army Recruiting Command utilized this C-12C (serial number 76-22264). It was factory fresh when this photograph was taken in July 1976. *Author*

The United States Army Forces Command at Fort Bragg, North Carolina, is the operator of this C-12C (serial number 73-22251). They had the red carpet rolled out for a four-star general. *Author*

C-12C serial number 73-22252 was visiting Minneapolis on August 20, 1983. With markings of the United States Army, it was probably attached to the Pentagon in Washington, DC. *Author*

The US Army Corps of Engineers flew this C-12C to Bach, Netherlands, in November 1978 for a special mission. The C-12 easily crossed the Atlantic Ocean to Europe. *Author*

C-12C serial number 73-22554 (in 1980) has a red placard in the rear window, indicating the presence of a four-star general of the United States Army Forces Command. *Author*

The Ninth Infantry Division of Fort Lewis, Washington, operated this C-12C (serial number 77-22934) when it was photographed in April 1991. *Author*

TRADOC stands for United States Army Training and Doctrine Command. They utilized this C-12C (serial number 76-2254) seen in May 1986. *Author*

Serial number 77-22945 was built as a C-12A, but was later converted to C-12C standards. Eventually, all sixty A models were converted to the C model. The C-12As or C-12Cs replaced U-21s in various units and commands. *Author*

This C-12A was converted to a C-12C. It was operated by the 35th Airborne when photographed in September 1980. The King Air series (U-21s and C-12s) has been in continuous production since 1964—over fifty years! *Author*

Headquarters, United States Army Europe (HQUSAEUR) flew C-12C serial number 78-23127. The C-12 was perfect for a VIP, liaison, and utility modern support aircraft. *Author*

C-12C serial number 76-22560 belonged to the United States Army Forces Command based at Fort Bragg, North Carolina. This is a large command, and they have a fleet of C-12s readily available. *Author*

C-12A serial number 76-22555 was converted to C-12C standards. It was operated by the United States Readiness Command in this October 1984 photograph. *Author*

C-12D

The C-12D was identical to the C-12C, except a cargo door was added to the left side of the fuselage. This model is based on the Beechcraft Model A200CT. Another change was the provision of fifty-two US gallon auxiliary fuel tanks on each wingtip. Also added was high-flotation landing gear. Serial numbers range from 1978 through 1984 for the forty-six aircraft ordered.

The Army took delivery of forty C-12Ds with Pratt & Whitney PT-6A-41 engines of 850 hp each. The US Air Force took delivery of six C-12Ds. The last six Army

C-12Ds were delivered with -42 engines of the same horsepower rating and became known as C-12D1s.

The very first C-12D (serial number 78-23140) was assigned to the US Army Aviation Technical Test Center at Fort Rucker, Alabama, and was used for a variety of test programs, so it was assigned the designation JC-12D.

Beech C-12D serial number 82-23785 belonged to the Arkansas Army National Guard and was based at the state capital in Little Rock. Not all liaison or utility aircraft were painted in gloss colors; this one is painted in standard overall gray (FS36231). *Author*

Serial number 78-23140 was a newly constructed C-12D in this fall 1980 photograph. The C-12D was later converted to the RC-12D. No badges or unit markings were visible on this Huron. *Author*

C-12D serial number 78-23142 has no unit insignias or markings on it, so it is unknown who operated it. Most "front line" unit or command aircraft were overall gray. It also could have been operated by a "special" unit that valued secrecy. *Author*

C-12D serial number 82-23784 has no unit markings on it, but it is a factory fresh aircraft, since the photograph was taken in August 1983. *Author*

RC-12D

At least thirteen C-12Ds were converted to RC-12Ds; the serial numbers were spread over the 78- to 81- series. One RC-12D (80-23378) was converted back to C-12D standards. Five RC-12Ds went to the Israeli Defense Forces/Air Force.

The RC-12D was used to supplement the RU-21H, especially in Europe and South Korea. RC-12Ds were SEMA platforms with the Guardrail V (CRAZYHORSE) AN/URD-9A ELINT improved Guardrail V systems. This was a remotely controlled communications intercept and direction finding system. These RC-12Ds reported directly to tactical commanders and corps level officers. Also included were M130 chaff/flare dispensing systems, AN/APR-44 radar warning receiver, Carousel IV-E internal navigation system for highly accurate navigation, TSQ-105 integral signals processor, AN/ALQ-156 missile warning system, AN/ALQ-136 radar jammer, AN/ARW-83V5 airborne relay secure data link, and the AN/ALQ-162 defensive ECM pods for the wingtips. They were also equipped with TACAN systems. Externally, more than twenty black antennas of various sizes and shapes could be seen, making the RC-12D a spectacularly interesting-looking aircraft. Maximum takeoff weight increased to 14,200 pounds.

The RC-12D became the workhorse of the intelligence-gathering fleet for the Army, lasting many years. RC-12Ds were operated by the 1st, 2nd, and 3rd Military Intelligence Battalions.

In sequence with the previous photograph, the same RC-12D continues on its mission in 1984. The IMPROVED GUARDRAIL V antenna array was impressive. *Beech*

Flying over the rugged Western United States, this RC-12D (serial number 80-23377) displays its unique antenna array. The Huron had the improved GUARDRAIL V airborne electronic sensor equipment package. *Beech*

Another C-12D (April 24, 1982) that was converted to an RC-12D was serial number 78-23145. It had no markings or unit badges on it, just a plain C-12D. Maybe! *Author*

RC-12D 86-23640 is parked on a ramp in the Western United States in July 1983. Later this RC-12D was quietly obtained by Israel. *Author*

RU-21D serial number 81-23542 (Wiesbaden, Germany, in April 1989) was based in Wiesbaden, Germany, with the 1st Military Intelligence Battalion, which monitored East Germany and other Communist-aligned nations. *Author*

This RC-12D displays a wide array of signal antennas as it flies over the snow-covered Kansas prairie. The RC-12D is filled with either the GUARDRAIL V or CRAZY HORSE airborne electronic sensor system. *Beech*

Beech RC-12D serial number 80-23376 appeared at an air show in Europe in August 1988. The Huron was from the 1st Military Intelligence Battalion. The aircraft is now on display at the Army Aviation Museum at Fort Rucker, Alabama. *Author*

C-12F

The C-12E was a US Air Force model. The Army did not have any E models. The C-12F is a mixed Army, Navy, and Air Force model. When the US Air Force chose to replace their aging North American CT-39 Sabreliners, the Beech C-12F (Beech Model A200CT) was chosen as an Operational Support Aircraft (OSA). Beech received a contract for the lease of forty aircraft for a five-year period with an option on a further three-year lease and ultimate USAF purchase after eight years. The first C-12F was delivered in May 1984 to Scott AFB, Illinois.

The Army ordered twenty-one with serial numbers in the 85- to 87- range. Six of them went to the Army National Guard. Three more were ordered in 1994; these were standard VIP and staff support versions.

The US Navy ordered twelve C-12Fs but called them UC-12Fs. Two of these (BuNo 163563 and 163564) were converted to RC-12Fs with AN/APS-140/504 sea search radar and were operated by the Pacific Missile Range Facility at Naval Station Barking Sands, Kauai, Hawaii. These two RC-12Fs provided range surveillance and missile range clearance capabilities (making sure the range was clear of sea traffic and Russian trawlers during missile test firings).

In 2001, these two RC-12Fs were transferred to VRC-30 at NAS North Island, California. The radar and associated systems were all removed, and the aircraft were converted back to UC-12Fs.

The US Air Force later transferred most of their C-12Fs to the Army for fleet consolidation, so there are C-12F1s, C-12F2s, and C-12F3s from the three branches of the US military, because each branch had slightly different equipment onboard.

The New York Army National Guard proudly displays their new Beech C-12F (serial number 86-0085) at a 1988 air show. *Author*

The Puerto Rico Army National Guard operated this C-12F (serial number 85-1263). It is headquartered in San Juan. *Author*

RC-12G

There were no C-12Gs utilized by the Army, but there were RC-12G models based on the C-12D Beech Model A200CT. Three were built (80-23379, 80-23380, and 80-23372). They were very similar to the RC-12D, but they were equipped with the much improved AN/URR-75 CRAZYHORSE airborne radio direction finding equipment, which was capable of remote operations. The system was developed for the US Army Southern Command and was based in Panama for Central American operations.

RC-12G 80-23380 had all of its CRAZYHORSE equipment removed, which changed its designation to the one and only JRC-12G model. It was stationed at the US Army Aviation Technical Test Center (USAATTC) at Fort Rucker, Alabama. It is now assigned to the Redstone Test Center's Aviation Flight Test Directorate (AFTD) at Redstone Arsenal, Alabama. The JRC-12G is outfitted with supporting icing testing on aircraft pursuing icing certification. These tests are conducted in Duluth, Minnesota, usually in January and February.

The RC-12H model carried the GUARDRAIL COMMON SENSOR/System 3. Serial number 83-24317 flies over a lake in the Western United States in 1986. *Beech*

Beech RC-12G serial number 80-23379 used the "Crazyhorse" airborne electronic sensor system. It was one of three built. *Mitch Waldran*

RC-12H

Based on the RC-12D (Beech Model A200CT), the H model was equipped with the Guardrail/Common Sensor System -3 and AN/USD-9B signal intelligence system. The difference between the D and H models was the antenna array and wingtip pods. Six were built (84-24313 through 84-24318). All six RC-12Hs were delivered to the 3rd Military Intelligence Battalion in South Korea in October 1988.

In 1996, Advanced Quicklook and Communication High Accuracy Airborne Location System (CHAALS) were added to these RC-12Hs. The antenna array differed significantly from the RC-12D model.

C-12J

There was no *I* model, so that it would not be confused with the number *1*. The next was the C-12J, which was actually a Beech 1900C airliner. The airliner had a stretched fuselage of 57 ft. 10 in. The cabin was increased by about 30%, and winglets were fitted for better hot and high performance. Also, twin ventral strakes were added to improve directional stability. Maximum cruising speed was now 334 mph. A lot of regional commuter airlines utilized the Beech 1900C airliner, which could hold up to nineteen passengers. It first flew on September 3, 1982.

The US Air Force bought six of them with 1986 serial numbers. During 1997, two of the C-12Js (both serial

numbers were 86-008x) were transferred to the Army after the Air Force declared them "excess" to their needs. One was assigned to Japan and the other was assigned to Germany. Later the US Army bought one (96-0112). It was powered by two Pratt & Whitney PT-6A-67D engines with 1,279 hp each. The Army version had an aft cargo door on the left side of the fuselage.

RC-12K carried highly classified airborne electronic sensor system equipment, so fake serial numbers might have been utilized. U-2 and SR-71 surveillance aircraft did the same thing. Here 85-0152 is a correct serial number. *Gary Stedman*

The Beech RC-12K had a massive array of antennas of various sizes and shapes, as shown here in May 1997 (serial number 89-0270). *Author*

The airborne electronic sensor system called GUARDRAIL COMMON SENSOR/SYSTEM 4 is carried on board RC-12X serial number 85-0149. This is one of the latest developments of the long line of GUARDRAIL systems. *Mike Waldron*

The United States Army Aviation Technical Test Center (USAATTC) operates the JRC-12G (serial number 80-23380). The beautiful high-visibility red-and-white color scheme is used near Duluth, Minnesota, for icing tests. This aircraft replaced an earlier U-21A test aircraft (serial number 66-18008). Note the two spray canisters on each wingtip for spraying water into the air, which instantly becomes ice. *Author*

RC-12K

The designation RC-12K was assigned to nine aircraft with serials 85-50147 through 85-50155. They were ordered in October 1985. Since the electronic equipment onboard was highly classified at the time, these might be bogus serial numbers. At least three RC-12Ks were converted from C-12Ds. They are powered by two Pratt & Whitney PT-6A-67 engines with 1,100 hp each. The K model is the airborne collection component of the AN/URD-9D Guardrail/ Common Sensor System 4, developed from the RC-12H model. Also included in the electronic suite are the M-130 chaff/flare dispensers, the AN/ALQ-136 radar jammer, and the AN/ARP-44 radar warning receiver, among other electronic equipment. Israel also received at least one RC-12K. The RC-12K was also based on the Beech Model A200CT. More RC-12Ks might have been ordered by the Army, but that information remains classified.

The RC-12K also has the cargo door installed. Since the onboard equipment was fairly heavy, stronger landing gear was installed, along with the earliest use of a series of additional small vertical fins added to the bottom of the horizontal stabilizers for better directional stability. The external antenna array on the K model is massive.

In May 1991 some of these aircraft replaced Grumman RV-1D Mohawks with the 1st Military Intelligence battalion in Wiesbaden, Germany.

C-12L

Following the removal of CEFLT LANCER sensor equipment from the three RU-21Js, they were redesignated C-12Ls. They became just normal utility aircraft. They have been retired from military service, and all have been sold to the civilian market.

C-12M series

Six C-12Cs were taken over by the Department of Homeland Security and modified with maritime search radar. They were redesignated C-12Ms.

The US Navy bought twelve UC-12Ms—actually C-12Cs, but the Navy called them the M model (BuNos 163836 through 163847). The last two Navy UC-12Ms were modified as RC-12Ms as range support aircraft with AN/APS-140/505 sea search radar. They were assigned to the Pacific Missile Test Center.

The Army had no C-12Ms and never ordered any.

RC-12N

A total of fifteen C-12Fs (Beech Model A200CT) were converted to RC-12N configuration with new serial numbers in the 88- to 91- series. They were powered by two Pratt & Whitney PT-6A-67 engines of 1,100 hp each. They have four-bladed propellers. The prototype was converted from the ninth and last RC-12K (serial number 85-50155), which could be a bogus serial number.

The RC-12N is an RC-12K with extensive aircraft survivability equipment added, including several types of electronic countermeasures: the AN/APR-39 radar warning receiver; AN/APR-44 radar warning system; AN/ALQ-136, AN/ALQ-156, and AN/ALQ-162 countermeasure sets; and chaff/flare dispensers. The aircraft is the airborne component of the AN/USD-9C Guardrail/Common Sensor System 1. As with the RC-12Ks, the antenna system is massive.

Due to the classified nature of the aircraft and mission, not much is known of their activities in Operation Iraqi Freedom or in Afghanistan, but they were there. Basically, if a "bad guy" turned on his cell phone, US forces knew it.

RC-12N serial number 91-0516 in landing configuration with the landing gear and flaps down. All windows behind the cockpit were covered over except for two round portholes to the rear of the fuselage. *Gary Stedman*

Beech RC-12N serial number 89-0271 in landing configuration proudly displays its antenna array. The T-shaped antenna protruding from the rear of the aircraft pivots ninety degrees in flight to become vertical. If it is in the horizontal position, it means that plane is on the ground or landing. *Max Tribolet*

Beech RC-12N displays a massive array of different sizes and shapes of antenna. N models were converted from C-12Fs. They had four-bladed propellers and engines with over twice the horsepower of the original U-21As. The far aft T antenna is rotating to the vertical position. *Beech*

RC-12N serial number 89-0273 (on May 17, 2002, in the Western United States) taxis in after another successful mission. The extra-small rudder fins added to the bottom of the horizontal stabilizers helped in directional control for heavier loads of electronic equipment. *Author*

The GUARDRAIL COMMON SENSOR/System I was installed on this RC-12N in 1995. The antenna array is impressive. It was fine-tuned over the succeeding years, and some of the antennas were removed or changed. *Beech*

RC-12P

There is no O model (also based on the Beech Model A200CT), to avoid confusion with the number *0*. There were nine RC-12P models ordered, with serial numbers ranging from 91- to 93-. The prototype was converted from the ninth RC-12K. The RC-12P models are equipped with the Guardrail/Common Sensor System 2 and are almost identical to the RC-12N model, but the P model utilizes fiber-optic cabling, smaller and lighter wingtip pods, and a revised antenna configuration. Onboard processing equipment was also increased. The COMINT and DF components of the Guardrail system are replaced by digital equipment developed by the US Air Force's Lockheed U-2 Senior Smart program called Communications High Accuracy Airborne Location System (CHAAS) and CHAAS-X (exploitable).

This Beech RC-12P has a large sensor belly pod, but the pod's purpose or function is unknown. *Joe Roy*

In 1998, the RC-12P carried the GUARDRAIL COMMON SENSOR/ SYSTEM 2 airborne electronic sensor equipment. The antenna array has changed over the years as modifications to the system are updated. *Beech*

In Iraq an RC-12P of the 15th Military Intelligence Battalion utilizes a ground air conditioning unit to cool electrical equipment against the background of desert heat. Cooler equipment functioned much better. *Adam Cowen*

A detailed inspection of the left wingtip pod of Beech RC-12P serial number 92-13120 reveals a varied size and style of sensors. *Bill Spidle*

RC-12P serial number 89-0276 returns to Balad Air Base, Iraq, on July 21, 2004, after another surveillance mission. *Jim Gordon*

RC-12Q

The Army obtained three (serial numbers are 93-0697, 93-0699, and 93-0701) RC-12Qs identical to the RC-12P AN/USD-9E Guardrail/Common Sensor System 2, with the exception of a large radome mounted on top of the aircraft. Housed in this radome is the antenna for the AN/ARW-87 direct air-to-satellite relay system. They have all been converted to RC-12Xs.

RC-12P serial number 93-0697 was converted to an RC-12X. It is operated by B Company, 224th Military Intelligence Battalion. At one time B Company was the 138th Aviation Company (Radio Research). They also belonged to the 224th Aviation Battalion when they were stationed in Vietnam. *US Army*

Beech RC-12Q serial number 93-0701 returns from another mission of intelligence gathering. The most striking feature of the RC-12Q is the satellite communication radome on top of the fuselage. *Barry Somerville*

The Army obtained three RC-12Qs with an added AN/ARW-87 satellite communication antenna. The serial number has been censored. *Beech*

The antenna array occasionally changed according to new equipment, a change of equipment, or a modification. This Huron has a slightly different array than the RC-12Q in the photo to the left. *Beech*

The last of three RC-12Qs built (serial number 93-0701) at a US military base. *Beech*

C-12R

The Army ordered twenty-nine C-12Rs (Beech Model B200C) in the 92- to 95- serial number range. They were ordered for the Army Reserve Command and the Army National Guard for staff and VIP transportation. The C-12Rs are powered by two Pratt & Whitney PT-6A-42 engines with 850 hp each and four-bladed propellers. They were basically identical to the C-12F, but with state-of-the-art avionics of the time, including a multifunctional display/electronic flight instrumentation system, digital autopilot, and global positioning system.

C-12S

This is a single aircraft for the US Drug Enforcement Agency and is an off-the-shelf Beech King Air 350. It does not carry a military serial number, so it is not a military aircraft.

The design of the improved version of the Beech Model 200 began in August 1980. Beech redesigned the engine cowlings, a 5-in. forward extension of the leading edge of the wing, and a 5-in. forward extension of the propeller line. It is called Super King Air Model 350. It is 2 ft. 11 in. longer than previous models, and the wing is 3 ft. 5 in. wider and features winglets.

To clarify an almost duplicate mission situation between the US Air Force and the US Army, the Army calls their version of the EMARSS system the MC-12S, while the US Air Force calls their version the MC-12W Liberty. The *M stands for* "multiservice." In this case, it means the US Army and US Air Force. See the C-12W series for details of the almost duplicate MC-12S and MC-12W.

C-12T

Forty C-12F1, C-12F2, and C-12F3 models assigned to the Army National Guard around the country were modernized with Collins cockpit updates, including night vision goggles, an FDS-255 electronic flight instrumentation system, a TSACII traffic collision system, RDR2000 color weather radar, an FMS 800 flight management system, and AN/ARC-210 radios.

Then the aircraft were redesignated C-12Ts. They kept their old serial numbers.

C-12U

In March 2003, the remaining thirty-nine C-12Ts were equipped with global air traffic management systems and became the C-12U. This included the Collins Proline 4 integrated flight management system, FDS-255 electronic flight instrumentation system, enhanced ground proximity warning system, TCASII traffic collision avoidance system, WXR-850 color weather radar, cockpit voice recorder/flight data recorder, and AN/ARC-210 radios. The Army also upgraded twenty-three other C-12s to C-12U standards. The first C-12Us were assigned to the 204th Military Intelligence Battalion at Fort Bliss, Texas. These are used for military intelligence support by the 204th.

C-12V

The C-12V is an upgrade of the C-12R with a redesigned cockpit, including console display, dual FMS 3000 GPS navigation, TCASII, air traffic warning, and Terrain Avoidance Warning System (TAWS). It is unknown how many were upgraded.

At least six have been converted (serial numbers 10-0256 through 10-0261). The most significant upgrade the C-12V incorporates is the Proline 21 cockpit by Rockwell Collins.

C-12W series

The C-12W version is utilized by all three services of the US military. They are based on the Beech 350 King Air ER series of civilian aircraft. The US Air Force version is called MC-12W Liberty. The name comes from the mission Project Liberty. The US Navy's version is called UC-12W. The Navy has twelve of the C-12Ws, but they are for VIP and staff transportation. The Army's version is called the MC-12S. All are basically the same airframe and engines. The Air Force version (MC-12W) and the Army version (MC-12S) are almost identical, except for some smaller equipment. The Air Force calls their system MARSS (Medium Altitude Reconnaissance Surveillance System) and the Army calls their system EMARSS (Enhanced Medium Altitude Reconnaissance Surveillance System). They are almost identical, but slightly different to avoid "mission duplication."

The prototype was converted RC-12N serial number 92-13122. The need for the MC-12S was so great the first seven were individually converted from commercial users and new construction. The new MC-12S has winglets, a tall satellite communication housing on top of the fuselage, and long-range fuel tanks at the rear of the engine nacelles. The additional fuel tanks are engine nacelle extensions, giving the MC-12 an eight-hour flying endurance. It has more equipment and heavier sensors than the Predator UAV. The engines are two Pratt & Whitney PT-6A-60As with 1,050 hp each. The crew members are the pilot, copilot, SIGINT operator, and electro-optical systems operator.

During the 400,000 combat hours flown by Air Force MC-12Ws in Iraq and Afghanistan, the Beeches helped kill or capture more than 8,000 terrorists, discovered more than 650 weapons caches, helped divert convoys around improved explosive devices (IEDs), and saved hundreds of coalition lives.

At least forty-two MC-12Ws have been ordered by the Air Force; the number of Army MC-12Ss is unknown. They are presently still in production for the Army at Beech's Wichita plant in a low-rate initial production (LRIP) mode. Four were scheduled for 2014, and two more for the year 2015. The Army has need for about thirty-six of these EMARSS aircraft. The Army wants to replace the Guardrail system with the EMARSS aircraft.

The MC-12 and W models are the next generation C-12-based airborne intelligence collection, processing, and targeting support equipment. It is an airborne intelligence, surveillance, and reconnaissance system that includes communication intelligence (COMINT), aerial precision guidance (APG), and electrical, optical, full real-time motion video, and infrared sensors. It also includes satellite communications (SATCOM), additional communications equipment, and aircraft survivability equipment, including AN/AAR-557 common missile warning system, three improved countermeasure dispensers (ICMD), and AN/APR-39C. Also included are the AN/APX-1213 IFF system, AN/ARN-153 tactical navigation system, and an embedded GPS system. In addition, there is a full laser targeting designator, which works on targets for drone strikes or conventional air strikes from AH-64 Apaches or other military aircraft.

The RAF has five of this model and calls them Shadows. Canada is interested in obtaining some, and France is also interested in obtaining a few of these aircraft. These would be the sensor-type aircraft. The Iraqi Air Force has ordered six UC-12Ws as VIP versions. Saudi Arabia has taken delivery of two of this model, with four more on order. This would be the VIP type of aircraft.

One of the US Air Force MC-12Ws users was the 361st Expeditionary Reconnaissance Squadron, activated in May 2010 by the US Air Force. It was always equipped with the Beech MC-12W aircraft. This squadron concluded its operations in Afghanistan on September 1, 2014, as part of the American drawdown in that country. This squadron's MC-12Ws flew more than 25,000 sorties, totaling 115,000 combat flying hours in support of Operation Enduring Freedom. The intelligence, surveillance, and reconnaissance missions provided "over-watch" for more than 50,000 friendly forces and scanned about 8,100 miles of roads.

As the MC-12Ws return to the United States, it is still in question how many will be taken over or converted to US Army standards—the MC-12S. So far, an unknown number of the MC-12W fleet has been transferred to US Army control. This transfer allowed for no interruption of the ISR services in Afghanistan operations. By 2016, the Army had taken over the entire mission, and all assets may have been transferred. The Army will utilize some of these transferred MC-12Ws for special operations.

In order to "hide" these additional MC-12s from "inquiries," the US Army "civilianized" some, if not all, of these ex-Air Force Liberty aircraft. The camouflage schemes were replaced by civilian stripes and markings, including N number FAA civilian registrations. They now look like "normal" Beech King Airs with a few "bumps and bulges" on them. Could these aircraft now be utilized by other government agencies more easily (read CIA)? Could these aircraft now *not* be included in the American military withdrawals from the area? On March 5, 2016, one of these former MC-12Ws crashed in Iraq, making public this "program."

At the Paris Air Show, Beechcraft and L3 Corporation display the test aircraft for the MC-12S and MC-12W series. Easily seen are the extra-range, long-distance fuel tanks, which are actually engine nacelle extensions. Barely visible is the satellite communication radome on top of the fuselage, just above the words "Mission Integration." *Beech*

The cockpit instrument panel has changed and developed from the basic, round dial instruments of the late 1940s into the mostly all-glass instrument panels of the MC-12s of the early 2000s. *HQ, USAF*

The RAF version of the MC-12 is the Shadow R1; the R stands for reconnaissance. All RAF Shadow R1s belong to Number 14 Squadron. Shadow serial number ZZ416 is shown taxiing out at Coningsby. *K. Bell*

The Enhanced Medium Altitude Reconnaissance and Surveillance System (EMARSS) first flight on May 22, 2013. This is the Army version of the system. The almost identical system used in the US Air Force MC-12W Liberty is called MARSS, with the word "enhanced" added by the Army. *Beech*

Iraq bought six UC-12Ws and this is one of them. They are not equipped with the latest airborne electronic sensors; instead they are more utilitarian in their mission. *Beech*

Beech and the US Army worked very closely to keep the airframe up to date. For instance, the installation of winglets as shown. *K. Bell*

US Army flight operations usually shared air bases with the US Air Force and other foreign allies in Iraq. This RC-12 shares the ramp with a US Air Force C-130. *Gary Chambers*

Another RC-12 taxis out at Balad Air Base, Iraq, for a mission in 2004. The desert sand, heat, and wind sometimes took their toll on the surveillance equipment. *Gary Chambers*

An aerial view of Balad Air Base (in 2004), approximately forty miles north of Baghdad, Iraq, shows numerous Army Beech RC-12s and an MQ-5B Hunter ISR (intelligence, surveillance, and reconnaissance) UAW, plus support equipment. *Gary Chambers*

RC-12X

The C-12X is a modified version of the RC-12K, RC-12N, RC-12P, and RC-12Q, with cockpit upgrades to comply with global air traffic management requirements. This is an ongoing upgrade. Another needed upgrade was the full-motion real-time video that was included, a major modernization of the Guardrail system. The RC-12X includes expanded frequency range monitoring. They can also locate transmitters in stand-off or stand-on mode with an antenna array that is capable of locating emitters in a dense signal environment. The system is state-of-the-art airborne SIGINT technology. In January 2011, the Army took delivery of two of the fourteen planned RC-12Xs.

RC-12X serial number 92-13123 is a vastly improved and current surveillance aircraft. One notable change is the wingtip sensors, which have a new upper portion with dozens of new receptors. *Beech*

An Army Beech RC-12X with no serial numbers shown flies along, displaying its antenna array. *Beech*

Could it be that Beech is working on another advanced RC-12J model with very large wingtip sensors? Perhaps this model is being developed for European Air Forces. It utilized the Beech 1900 airliner airframe for more capacity. *Beech*

RC-12X serial number 92-13122 lands at Mindenhall, United Kingdom, on December 17, 2010. It is difficult to tell the most recent versions of the RC-12 series of aircraft because the equipment and antenna arrays change occasionally. *K. Bell*

APPENDIX

C-45 EXPEDITOR Specifications

Crew: 2
Accommodations: up to 6
Power Plant: (2) Pratt & Whitney R-985-AN-14B radial piston engines (336 kW) 450 hp
Wingspan: 50.7 ft. (15.15 m)
Length: 35.2 ft. (10.73 m)
Height: 9.3 ft. (2.84 m)
Maximum speed: 220 mph (354 km/h)
Cruise speed: 185 mph (300 km/h)
Ceiling: 21,400 ft. (6,525 m)
Range: 700–1,400 miles (1,125–2,253 km)
(depending on version of C-45 series)

T-42A Specifications

Crew: 1
Capacity: 5
Length: 28 ft. (8.53 m)
Wingspan: 37 ft. 10 in (11.53 m)
Height: 9 ft. 7 in (2.92 m)
Empty weight: 3,156 lb. (1,431 kg)
Max. takeoff weight: 5,100 lb. (2,313 kg)
Power Plant: (2) Continental IO-470-L air-cooled,
6-cylinder, horizontally opposed piston engines of 260 hp (194 kW) each
Maximum speed: 236 mph (205 knots) (380 km/h)
Cruise speed: 207 mph (180 knots) (333 km/h)
Range: 942 nautical miles (1,746 km) (1,085 miles)
Service ceiling: 19,700 feet (6,000 m)

U-21 UTE Specifications

Crew: 2
Accommodations: 2 to 10
Length: 35.5 ft. (10.82 m)
Wingspan: 50.26 ft. (15.32 m)
Height: 14.24 ft. (4.34 m)
Empty weight: 6,945 lb. (3,150 kg)
Takeoff weight: 10,097 lb. (4,580 kg) (U-21A, B, C, D, H)
11,500 lb. (5,730 kg) (U-21F)
14,500 lb. (6,591 kg) (U-21J)
Power Plant: (2) Pratt & Whitney Canada PT-6A-20
550 hp (U-21A, B, C, D, H)
(2) Pratt & Whitney Canada PT-6A-28
680 hp (U-21F)
(2) Pratt & Whitney Canada PT-6A-42
850 hp (U-21J)
Maximum speed: 311 mph (500 km/h) (270 kts)
Cruising speed: 190 mph
Range: 1,520 miles (2,446 km)
Ceiling: 30,000 ft. (9,144 m)
Rate of climb: 2,000 feet per minute (610 m/min)

C-12 HURON Specifications

Crew: 2
Accommodations: up to 14
Power Plant: (2) Pratt & Whitney Canada PT-6A-38 turboprop engines 750 hp (560 kW)
(2) Pratt & Whitney Canada PT-6A-42 turboprop engines 850 hp (634kW) (C-12C, D, F, G, H, M, R, T, U, V)
(2) Pratt & Whitney Canada PT-6A-67 turboprop engines 1,100 hp (821kW) (C-12K, L, N, P, Q, X)
(2) Pratt & Whitney Canada PT-6A-67D turboprop engines 1,279 hp (955 kW) (C-12J)
(2) Pratt & Whitney Canada PT-6A-60A turboprop engines 1,050 hp (785 kW)
Wingspan: 57.9 ft. (17.65 m)
Length: 46.7 ft. (14.22 m)
Height: 14.3 ft. (4.37 m)
Takeoff weight: 12,500 lb. (5,669 kg) (non-SEMA)
Takeoff weight: 14,200 lb. (RC-12D, H)
Takeoff weight: 16,000 lb. (RC-12K, N, P)
Takeoff weight: 16,500 lb. (MC-12W)
Empty weight: 7,537 lb. (3,419 kg) (non-SEMA)
Maximum speed: 339 mph (545 km/h) (non-SEMA)
Maximum speed: 285 mph (312 kts) (MC-12W)
Range: 2,334 miles (3,756 km) (non-SEMA)
Range: 2,200 miles (MC-12W)
Ceiling: 35,000 ft. (10,670 m)
Endurance: 5+ hours